The Body in
Hollywood Slapstick

The Body in Hollywood Slapstick

ALEX CLAYTON

McFarland & Company, Inc., Publishers
Jefferson, North Carolina, and London

LIBRARY OF CONGRESS CATALOGUING-IN-PUBLICATION DATA

Clayton, Alex.
The body in Hollywood slapstick / Alex Clayton.
p.   cm.
Includes bibliographical references and index.

ISBN-13: 978-0-7864-3063-5
softcover : 50# alkaline paper ∞

1. Comedy films — United States — History and criticism.
2. Body, Human, in motion pictures.   I. Title.
PN1995.9.C55C58 2007
791.43'6170973 — dc22   2007015420

British Library cataloguing data are available

On the cover: Buster Keaton and Margaret Leahy in a publicity
still from *Three Ages*, 1923; *(inset)* Buster Keaton demonstrates
his "flogged-piston sprint"

Manufactured in the United States of America

McFarland & Company, Inc., Publishers
 Box 611, Jefferson, North Carolina 28640
 www.mcfarlandpub.com

Acknowledgments

Thank you to the Arts and Humanities Research Council for supporting me financially throughout the project. Warm thanks to Andrew Klevan for his criticisms and insight, to Dave Turner for his advice and support, to Sarah Moore for her patience and care — and to Charles Chaplin, Buster Keaton, Stan Laurel and Oliver Hardy for making some of the best films I've ever seen.

Contents

Preface

This book is an exploration and, ultimately, a celebration of the Hollywood genre of physical comedy from the silent era onwards. As such, it is aimed at both the scholar interested in film comedy and the non-professional enthusiast. I know of no good reason why a book shouldn't be written in a way that can appeal to both kinds of people. I would even say that film studies has a duty to communicate beyond the campus and classroom.

At any rate, I consider myself a fan of this comedy as well as one of its students. Like many others, I grew up with precious glimpses on TV of Laurel and Hardy, and, like just about everyone I know, I fell in love with the way they were with one another on screen. Here was an image of friendship with all its pitfalls and in all its glory, and what made it so charming and so funny was the sheer *physicalness* of it all: Ollie and Stan, one fat, one thin, quaking at the knees on a mile-high scaffold, laughing uncontrollably at nothing in particular, kicking each other in the shins or rump and making a beeline for the horizon, the fat one after the thin one, as the film drew to a close. I also recall a cartoon version, probably made cheaply in the 1970s, which had none of the verve or the charm or the laughs. While there were no doubt lots of reasons for this felt deficiency, one reason may have been that what made the films feel more alive was the vividness of the bodies involved, inhabiting spaces with a real-world weight and possessing physical attributes that were generally rooted in an everyday

1

experience of one's own and others' bodies (I recall Ollie kneeling up from a crouching position and thumping his head on a sock drawer thoughtlessly left open by Stan).

What I want to do in this book is to reinvigorate a sense of that physicality and argue for the significance of bodily experience in film, in comedy and, by implication, in everyday life. My feeling is that the comedies discussed in this book make such a case for themselves in their own distinctive ways. I hope that I manage to urge readers to rediscover some of them.

In addition, the book explores comic performance through accounts of gestures, postures and positioning, moment-by-moment, in what I take to be exemplary (in the double sense of being characteristic *and* exceptional) moments from the genre. This is the best way I know of getting at the detail, hence the significance of particular performances and films. The business of selection (i.e., of selecting particular moments from particular films), when made overt in this way, always runs the risk that the writer will be accused of being partial in the treatment — partial in the sense of dealing only with part of a larger picture, and also of unduly favoring certain things, in this case certain performers and films. Here a few words to defend myself against these invented accusations. I make no claims that what I write in this book is definitive in the sense of wrapping up the case, once and for all. I hope my accounts strike readers as appropriate, without being overbearing and possessive of the films, and that my book urges readers to explore other related areas of the larger picture, whatever that may be.

Against the potential accusation that I unduly favor, say, films featuring Buster Keaton and Jerry Lewis over, say, films featuring the Three Stooges and Danny Kaye, I offer no apology or excuse, except to say that I do not think my preference undue because I have generally chosen performers and films that I take to represent the best the genre has to offer, and have implied reasons for the selection in each case. I am always open to (in fact, would welcome) the appeal that other important films and performers have been overlooked or neglected in my study, unfairly for this or that reason. (Likewise a reasoned appeal that a performer has been overpraised: coming from the United Kingdom, I am led to believe that the mere inclusion of Jerry Lewis along-side the names of those more widely accepted as great comic performers, such as Charlie Chaplin and Harold Lloyd, is likely to raise eyebrows in some quarters of the United States. I hope I have justified the inclusion sufficiently.)

The book is arranged into chapters dealing with a particular relationship between the body and something else: clothes, self, voice, pain, and so on. This seemed a logical structure since I wanted to stress the idea that the body (in these films as in lived experience) is never cordoned off discretely from other elements, and that it is always situated in relation to something else. The list of relationships I discuss is by no means exhaustive, but addressing the body in this way seemed an effective path into analyzing and appreciating the qualities of these films. Since almost all films prominently feature human bodies, I believe this approach may be fruitfully employed as a way of analyzing and appreciating other types of movies.

So much of what is written about the body in academic circles is obscure and abstract, often seemingly divorced from actual bodily experience. I wanted to write about the body in more concrete, everyday language, while remaining open to its curiousness and to philosophical ideas about the body. Similarly, I wanted to write about comedy in a way that did not kill it off, but kept it alive, perhaps even vivified it in a new way. I leave it to others to decide if I have achieved this. I hope you enjoy the book.

Charlie Chaplin as the Tramp.

Introduction: The Body in Hollywood Slapstick

Anatomy of a Comic Turn

Few gestures have been as celebrated — or as imitated — as those of Charlie Chaplin's Tramp. His waddling walk and the dog-like way he stretches his legs; his expressive facial wiggles, accentuated by darkened brows and an absurd brush moustache; his peculiar method of navigating corners at speed, by hopping on one foot and jutting out the other at an angle: the continued power of such iconic gestures to provoke laughter and inspire wonder is testament to the vividness with which they are enacted on film. They seem to capture something about the human condition, at once mysterious and plain to see. What is it about his way of booting away the core of an apple, for instance, by tossing it over his shoulder and kicking his leg up and out to the side, that seems such a marvelous discovery? Is it the luxurious nonchalance with which he dispenses with the object? Is it the combination of balletic grace and childlike cheekiness? Does it lie in our grasp that the gesture is performed for nobody and everybody, at once precious and throwaway? A shared sense of its power and significance can only be achieved by returning to the precise details of the moment, and of all comic performers we might say that Chaplin is foremost in calling for, and rewarding, our absolute attention to the minutiae of physical movement: blink and you'll miss the fleeting twitch, twist or glance that captures his outlook. It is this close and sustained attention to the body — as a medium of expression, but also crucially, as a body — that I propose to undertake in this book, as I seek to explore the deployment and presentation of the body in the Hollywood genre of slapstick comedy.[1]

A brief analysis of two contrasting instances of turning, as performed in each case by Charlie Chaplin, should serve to suggest the value of attending to the precise details of a performer's physicality. In the opening sequence of *Shoulder Arms* (1918), Charlie is a new recruit to the army, standing to attention at the end of a line of soldiers, each of whom rests a rifle against his right shoulder. Despite wearing the same uniform as the other rank-and-file soldiers, however, Charlie is immediately set apart from the others by the particular way he inhabits his outfit: his trousers bagging out a little too much at the thighs, his tight jacket accentuating the effeminate slightness of his build, his felt hat slightly squashed in at the top with the brim raised up like a sunhat. Whereas the other soldiers stand upright in the formal stance with their legs together and their feet pointing forwards, Charlie's feet point gawkily outwards to each side, and, in an over-eager effort to stand rigidly straight, his back is curved inward and his pelvis thrown forward. The difference becomes yet more marked when the men are commanded to bring their rifles down, and, with appropriate gusto but inappropriate delivery, Charlie thrusts down the butt of his gun to the wrong side, and onto the toe of his nearest neighbor (who grabs his foot in pain and irritation, his reflexive response breaking the formation for a moment). The soldiers are commanded to "about-turn," and while all the other men execute a swift maneuver by placing one foot behind the other and spinning clockwise briskly on the ball of that foot, Charlie's turn is not so slick. Vigorously swiveling his hips to twist the rest of his legs a quarter-turn anti-clockwise (wrong way again!), he then requires a repetition of the swiveling motion to complete the full turn. The Colonel singles him out for correction, and asks him to do it again. Charlie complies and performs the same movement, more briskly but with an equally ungainly result. The repetition

6

A cheeky stage curtsy from *Shoulder Arms* (1918).

allows us to see how the inelegance of this wiggling movement is produced by the way Chaplin keeps his feet at right angles to one another, and to recognize this curious method of turning as, in fact, a creative solution to the problem of how to turn right around while keeping one's heels together. The joke here thus rests on the stubborn inflexibility of Charlie's body in relation to the ingenuity of his approach.

The Colonel proceeds to show how it *should* be done, and directs Charlie to copy the starting position of placing one foot behind the other. But Charlie's adoption of the posture, executed with a little hop and a hand placed daintily out to the side, transforms it into a sort of stage curtsy, and he grins at the colonel as if for approval. In brazenly drawing out the connection between a military maneuver and an effete theatrical flourish, the performer's self-consciousness steps forward for an instant through the character's cheekiness. Suddenly Charlie's body becomes capable of a nimble and delicate gesture under the very pretext of his not being able to control his body, an observation that only heightens its audacity. Chaplin's self-consciousness here draws attention to the dexterity of acting out clumsiness, to the skill of appearing inept. With his feet now crossed, Charlie's attempt to execute the about-turn is at once agile and maladroit. Continuing to swivel at the hips, he now appears off balance and unable to complete the move. In an accomplished piece of clowning, Chaplin creates the impression of a body completely tied in knots, with his hips, head and crossed feet all seeming to squirm autonomously from one another with the effort to twist himself around. Ironically, the Colonel's effort to straighten out Charlie's body has only served to exacerbate his inflexibility.

A different type of turning can be found in *The Circus* (1928). Having been accused of stealing a wallet at a circus sideshow, Charlie tries to evade the cops by disguising himself as a mechanical figure on the side of the fairground fun-house. As the policemen scout for a fleeing figure, Charlie stands stock-still on the upper tier gallery, clutching his cane tightly in one hand, and rigidly twists his body back and

Charlie disguised as a mechanical figure in *The Circus* (1928).

forth at set intervals of time. With his feet hidden from view, so that no part of his body seems to be moving independently, the movement appears perfectly mechanical, as if he were pivoting to and fro on a simple axis. He even captures the slight quiver of inert matter as it snaps into position each time.

In *Shoulder Arms*, Charlie's unorthodox execution of the turn offered a miniature protest against the idea of the regimented body, divorced from reflex and drained of individuality; but in *The Circus*, it is precisely the adoption of a slick, swift turn — methodical, precise and consistent — that allows Charlie to keep his freedom.[2] With this consummate depiction of lifelessness, Charlie realizes a camouflage that could not have been achieved had he tried to scamper away. Moreover, in a film expressly interested in the ambiguities of what constitutes a performance,[3] we are offered here a type of performance that is designed to go entirely unnoticed by the audience at hand. In *Shoulder Arms*, Charlie's body is made to demonstrably stand out from the other soldiers (a conspicuous conspicuousness given his later proficiency behind enemy lines when he disguises himself as a tree). In *The Circus*, the audacity of the performance, and his commitment to it, shields him from detection. Both sequences foreground the act of performance — at turns self-conscious, unobtrusive, ostentatious, ineffectual, dexterous — and crucially revolve around the matter of visibility. The choice of fairly distanced camera placements in each instance is thus important not because this decision is expressive in itself, but because it offers us the best possible position from which to view Chaplin's performance, to see his whole body move and react in its context. In the sequence from *The Circus*, Chaplin alternates between a far shot of the fun house, allowing us to see Charlie's automaton *in relation* to the searching cops and the other mechanical figures on the fun house, and a medium shot that offers a slightly closer inspection of Charlie's proficient performance, while maintaining a sufficient distance to keep his whole body in frame and his camouflage amusingly credible. In the scene from *Shoulder Arms*, presented as a single, unbroken medium-far shot, Chaplin's refusal of the opportunity to cut to a series of close ups of the fumbled turn means that we can see the *relation* between his hips, head and feet as he squirms himself into a human knot. In each case, the undeclamatory camera style puts the emphasis squarely on the details of physical performance, on the movements of the human body in its immediate and defining context.

Chaplin's unwillingness to gratuitously isolate the body should alert us to an important insight that is pertinent to this study: namely, that the body should not be considered as if it were an utterly discrete element. This extends beyond the important point that physical performance should not be unduly divorced from other aspects of the film's construction (framing, costume, editing, and so on), or from a broader appreciation of the film's style, tone and range of meanings. It should lead us to the recognition that the body is never *simply* a body, but exists in relation to other elements, not least (unless we are to reduce human beings to walking corpses) in relation to the particular personality, self or mind of whoever's body it happens to be. As such, it can bear an especially intimate and variable relation to features such as the voice and feelings of pain. Moreover, an individual body is seen to inhabit, and interact within, a particular social and physical universe. It operates in relation to specific social expectations and norms, such as those pertaining to gender, and in relation to objects with which it can manifest an unusual affinity, such as clothes or machines. I hope to have suggested a number of these relationships to be pertinent in my descriptions of the two sequences offered above. This understanding of the body, as always operating in a dynamic relationship with other elements, shapes the overall structure of this book. Each chapter in turn examines the body in relation to a specific other element: Body and Mind, Body and World, Body and Clothes, Body and Machine, Body and Frame, Body and Voice, Body and Gender, Body and Pain, Body and Self. Such a structure should enable a more insightful understanding of the *place* of the body than an isolating perspective might allow for.

Film and the Physicality of Physical Comedy

The body is a natural subject for film because of the photographic basis of its visual field. For the medium of film, as distinct from other

10

narrative arts such as literature or animation, the body is not described or drawn, but photographed and projected. The directness of this process might lead us to say that in movies the human figure is not so much represented as *presented*. Such a claim does not deny, of course, the important contributions of make up, costume or prosthetic limbs for modifying the body's appearance, nor the possibilities of cutting and framing for presenting the body in countless different ways, nor the potential of slow motion or freeze frame for varying the rate of its projection. Such techniques are methods of presentation, but pointing to such methods cannot disavow the fact of their presentation by means of mechanical reproduction. This dimension of film has been explored and celebrated by theorists such as André Bazin and Stanley Cavell, each of whom stresses the automatism of cinema's reproduction of the world (that is, the way it bypasses the human hand in the creation of its forms).[4] Such an emphasis should allow us to appreciate the precise sense in which we might say the body is *presented*, rather than created or constructed, in the medium of film. To emphasize this dimension is to insist upon the physicality of the characters that populate movies, and hence upon the lived body as inexorably central to film's depiction of human beings.

The promise of movies to exhibit the human figure in motion, grasped at least as far back as Eadweard Muybridge's sequential photographs of human beings running and walking, continues to hold a mysterious fascination over us.[5] This promise is a determining feature of the slapstick form, which, along with the action movie and the dance musical, is foremost in exploiting cinema's potential to exhibit the moving body as such. Indeed, the energy, vigor and violence of slapstick comedy (of human bodies running and tumbling and being kicked in the pants, for instance) can itself be seen as a declaration of the physicality of its objects and people. When David (Cary Grant) enters the frame by slipping on an olive in *Bringing Up Baby* (1938), the force with which he hits the ground is undeniably the force of a real grown man, of precisely Grant's size and shape, falling with a thwump to the floor. It *is* Cary Grant who has fallen, awakening his character from the heaviness of private contemplation by establishing his physical

Cary Grant slips on an olive in *Bringing Up Baby* (1938); Katharine Hepburn reacts.

weight, projecting him into the world of strident play that Katharine Hepburn so arrestingly embodies. And just as Grant's character is drawn into a physical universe, the brutal force of a slapstick pratfall has the capacity to reawaken us to the fundamental physicality of the world, and hence to its detail: to its textures and rhythms, to relationships elemental and vivid, to the momentary triumphs and failures of human endeavor, to the incongruity and rightness of certain actions and gestures, to the physical laws and properties that restrict and permit human activity. Ironically, the very brutality of slapstick has the potential to engender a heightened sensitivity to the world.

To acknowledge that the body that falls is that of a real human being is to recognize the fact that characters on film are embodied. This is a feature that cartoon representations of human beings cannot truly be said to possess. (If we want to say that Elmer Fudd is embodied, this would be an odd way of stating that his shape resembles human form; human characters on film, by contrast, whatever they are, are not the mere *likeness* of human beings.) The complex and ever-shifting relationship between the character and the performer is an endlessly intriguing puzzle, and one that seems vital to recognize in a study of the body in movies. Whose body is it, for instance, that slips on an olive and falls to the floor? I have already said: it is Cary Grant's. But it is also David's body, otherwise Susan (Katharine Hepburn) would not greet him as such. Yet there is only one figure to point at, as with Wittgenstein's duck-rabbit. We might draw out the distinction along the lines of intention: David did not *mean* to fall over, at least not consciously, whereas Cary Grant did. (We might confidently assume this from what we know about actors in movies, and from the set-up of the pratfall, with the camera waiting for Grant's entrance into the frame to perform the required stunt.) With this in mind, we might point out that Grant's body is remarkably agile, whereas David's is remarkably clumsy. But we are still talking about the same body, are we not?

The ever-present possibility of slipping on an olive is a condition of being embodied, something we all have to learn to live with. Embodiment, in this sense, suggests nothing more, or less, than the fact of having, or being, a body. When we say that characters on film are embodied by performers, we mean something slightly different but importantly related. By exploring how the body is presented and deployed in the genre of Hollywood slapstick, and by evoking the detail of performance, I hope to illustrate how the condition of embodiment constitutes one of the genre's major subjects.

The Comic Body: Bergson, Freud, Bakhtin

Much theoretical discussion of comedy has focused on the question of what makes us laugh. There are a number of reasons why the pursuit of an answer to that question is not a priority of this book. The production of laughter is obviously importantly bound up with the explicit aims of comedy, but that connection should not be confused with its being synonymous with comedy's achievements. This is a particular temptation when considering Hollywood slapstick because of the intensity of laughter it can provoke.[6] But just as the quality of a Max Ophuls or Douglas Sirk melodrama is rightly not judged on the basis of the volume of tears produced at its finale (which is not to say that Ophuls and Sirk were uninterested in soliciting an empathetic response), laughter is not an index of comic achievement. That the seriousness of Buster Keaton's face should be able to prompt uncontrollable guffaws *and* quiet awe should not be held against him. Although asking oneself the question, "What caused me to laugh there?" often proves a very instructive place to start, an over-emphasis on the matter of "what makes it funny" will lead to a distorted view of the achievements of slapstick comedy. Nevertheless, some theoretical investigations into the subject of laughter and the nature of the comic have yielded important insights that might help with a study of comedy. At this juncture, I wish merely to outline three contrasting accounts of the comic body in the work of three major theorists. While none of these accounts may satisfy our sense of the complexity and variety of the presentation of the body in Hollywood slapstick, each offers something like a paradigm from which we might advance a consideration of the topic.

Henri Bergson's understanding of the comic provides quite a useful framework for thinking about the role of the body in film comedy. Bergson points out that the comic experience often gains its force from the way it draws attention to the very physical substance of the body, which in other circumstances we are apt to overlook. Evidently this observation chimes with our understanding of Cary Grant's pratfall in *Bringing Up Baby* as a declaration of his physicality. But Bergson's explanation proposes a further dimension to such an incident:

> When we see only gracefulness and suppleness in the living body, it is because we disregard in it the elements of weight, of resistance, and, in a word, of matter; we forget its materiality and think only of its vitality, a vitality which we regard as derived from the very principle of intellectual and moral life. Let us suppose, however, that our attention is drawn to this material side of the body; that, so far from sharing in the lightness and subtlety of the principle with which it is animated, the body is no more in our eyes than a heavy and cumbersome vesture, a kind of irksome ballast which holds down to earth a soul eager to rise aloft.[7]

14

By calling attention to the materiality of the body, a comic incident reveals, for Bergson, a fundamental incongruity within the human subject. Drawing on the metaphor of weight and traditional Christian imagery of the spirit eager to rise to heaven, Bergson paints that incongruity as a conflict between body and soul. The body is revealed as "heavy and cumbersome," a burden that holds us back: hence the comic appearance of clumsiness, rigidity and unthinking momentum, where the body stubbornly takes control. "[The] soul imparts a portion of its winged lightness to the body it animates: the immateriality which thus passes into matter is what is called gracefulness," he writes. "Matter, however, is obstinate and resists. It draws to itself the ever-alert activity of this higher principle, would fain convert it to its own inertia and cause it to revert to mere automatism."[8] The appearance of such inertia and automatism provokes laughter because it reveals "a certain rigidity of body, mind and character that society would still like to get rid of in order to obtain from its members the greatest possible degree of elasticity and sociability. This rigidity is the comic, and laughter is its corrective."[9] Hence, for Bergson, "the attitudes, gestures and movements of the human body are laughable in exact proportion as that body reminds us of a mere machine."[10]

Such a statement might immediately call to mind Chaplin's automaton, twisting back and forth on the front of the fairground fun-house. Yet even this apparently exemplary case should immediately prompt us to question Bergson's line of argument. Charlie's appearance perfectly resembles a mechanical figure, operating involuntarily and with the rigidity of inert matter. Yet such rigidity can in no way be thought to represent an absent-minded clumsiness, or an involuntary reversion to inertia. Indeed, it is precisely the result of a remarkable *elasticity* of mind and body: who else would think to disguise himself in this way, and could attain it with such swiftness and precision? Bergson's abstraction of the comic device forces the overly schematic assertion, but by virtue of its very bluntness the suggestion still may serve as a useful paradigm of what the comic body *might* look like, in order that we might refine our understanding of the specific instance. Bergson's contention will be taken up again and the body-machine relation explored at greater length in Chapter 4.

Sigmund Freud's notable contribution to comic theory, *The Joke and Its Relation to the Unconscious*, concentrates primarily on verbal rather than physical humor, but offers some thoughts on what he calls the "comedy of movement" in the chapter entitled "The Joke and Varieties of the Comic." Freud wonders why it is that we tend to find amusing a certain type of disproportionate and impracticable movement, such as certain exaggerated gestures of clowns and mimes that suggest an "over-great expenditure"; or "when a child is trying to write and stretches out his tongue to follow the movements of the pen"; or "a skittle-player after he has thrown the ball, following its course as if he could control it in retrospect"; or someone who is able to "waggle their ears."[11] Freud's explanation is that the amused onlooker is somehow involved in a course of comparison between themselves and the other person. A sort of "mimicry of the imagination" takes place, Freud argues, wherein the onlooker is engaged in an unconscious comparison between the movement observed and the movement he or she would have performed in their place; the larger the discrepancy, the greater the surplus "expenditure of energy" on the part of the onlooker, which, Freud suggests, might manifest itself as laughter.[12] However, Freud rejects the idea that this comic feeling is simply the result of a feeling of superiority, or *schadenfreude*, which he understands as more characteristic of children's laughter, a laughter of "pure pleasure," ridicule and self-satisfaction derived from knowing how to perform the action better. Indeed, adults, by contrast, seem to have lost this capacity for pure pleasure and instead the 'comic feeling' arises as something of a substitute for that loss. As Freud writes,

> If one might generalize, it would appear very tempting to relocate the specific characteristics of the comic that we are looking for to the revival of the child in us, and understand the comic as the "lost laughter of childhood" regained. We could then say: I always laugh at a difference in expenditure between another person and myself whenever I rediscover the child in the other. Or, more precisely, the full comparison leading to a [feeling for] the comic would run:
> That's how he does it — I do it differently —
> He does it in the way I used to do it as a child.[13]

By extension, then, at least in the genre of what Freud calls the "comedy of movement" (which might be considered closely related to the slapstick form), the comic body is understood as the means of activating such a comparison between the self-as-adult and the self-as-child: an adult body that recalls childish behavior or childlike states, not simply by mimicking a child, but by "touching on children's nature generally, perhaps even on children's suffering."[14] (Freud notes that no such comic impression arises when children themselves are the object of the comparison, which he explains by pointing out that in such an instance the comparison is more overt and so does not operate at a preconscious level.) The immediate performer that comes to mind given Freud's association is Harry Langdon (discussed in Chapter 3 of this book), although we might well discover *threads* of such a paradigm in all the major slapstick performers. Keeping such a paradigm in mind might allow for a different understanding of the pratfall, for instance, as a loss of bodily control that recalls the experience of precariousness as a

child, and so might alert us to elements of the fall that proficiently achieve such an impression. Again, as with Bergson's paradigm, we should welcome the definite perspective offered by comic theory, but be careful to acknowledge the limits of such a generalized picture. It might, of course, be more significant to recognize the way Grant's pratfall in *Bringing Up Baby* recalls peculiarly *adult*-like states — say, the loss of dignity in an urbane setting — than the way it may touch on children's nature or movement.

Harry Langdon: half-man, half-child, half-loopy.

The final work I want to

make reference to in noting some paradigms of the comic body is Mikhail Bakhtin's influential and important study on the literature of François Rabelais, in its relation to the carnival culture of the Middle Ages. In the chapter entitled "The Grotesque Image of the Body and Its Sources," Bakhtin sets out the conception of the body underpinning medieval folk humor and the comic literature of Rabelais:

> The grotesque body ... is a body in the act of becoming. It is never finished, never completed.... This is why the essential role belongs to those parts of the grotesque body in which it outgrows its own self, transgressing its own body, in which it conceives a new, second body: the bowels and the phallus.... Next to the bowels and the genital organs is the mouth, through which enters the world to be swallowed up. And next is the anus. All these convexities and orifices have a common characteristic; it is within them that the confines between bodies and between the body and the world are overcome: there is an interchange and an interorientation. This is why the main events in the life of the grotesque body, the acts of the bodily drama, take place in this sphere. Eating, drinking, defecation and other elimination (sweating, blowing of the nose, sneezing), as well as copulation, pregnancy, dismemberment, swallowing up by another body ... in all these events the beginning and the end of life are closely linked and interwoven.[15]

Bakhtin's study sketches a particular conception of the body that emphasizes and celebrates the body's incompleteness, its interchange with the world via the orifices of mouth and anus, its protrusions in the form of the belly, nose and buttocks. The lower bodily stratum is especially stressed and elevated above all else, as if to echo the topsy-turvy world of carnival's inversion of hierarchy. An easy passage between inside and outside (as when, in *Pantagruel*, King Anarchus is described as having "barely swallowed one spoonful [of syrup laced with red pepper] when a terrific burning seared his mouth, ulcerated his uvula and peeled the whole surface of his tongue"[16]) blurs the sense of a bounded, individuated body. Indeed, the imagery of Rabelais' literature conveys a body that is neither discrete nor discreet. The activities brought to the fore in nonofficial carnival culture, such as Bakhtin lists above (with some relish!), are precisely those that the official feudal and ecclesiastical culture of the medieval period, as well as polite society of our own time, has sought to moderate or disguise. The presentation of the body in official culture (what Bakhtin calls the "new bodily canon") is in fact diametrically opposed to the grotesque body of folk culture:

> The new bodily canon, in all its historic variations and different genres, presents an entirely finished, completed, strictly limited body, which is shown from the outside as something individual. That which protrudes, bulges, sprouts, or branches off (when a body transgresses its limits and a new one begins) is eliminated, hidden or moderated. All orifices of the body are closed. The basis of the image is the individual, strictly limited mass, the impenetrable façade.... In the new canon, such parts of the body as the genital organs, the buttocks, belly, nose and mouth cease to play the leading role ... [which is instead] attributed to the individually characteristic and expressive parts of the body: the head, face, eyes, lips, to the muscular system, and to the place of the body in the external world.... The body of the new canon is merely one body: no signs of duality have been left.[17]

The dichotomy Bakhtin sketches between two conceptions of the body is useful for a consideration of how the body is presented in a genre (and medium) that postdates medieval folk culture, but contains at least a trace of its tenor. We might find *threads* of the grotesque body in a range of slapstick performers,[18] but we should be careful not to overstate the case if we want to remain faithful to the films and to our experience.[19] Indeed, we might equally, in fact more easily, find threads of the official "bodily canon," as outlined by Bakhtin, in the same range of performers' work. It might be that the camera's recording of exterior surfaces naturally places film on the side of the divide that stresses the boundedness of the body, rather than its openings. Hollywood slapstick seems especially interested in the "place of the body in the external world," indeed draws much of its humor from this condition. Yet slapstick *does* dwell on certain protrusions and orifices, and the activity of eating is particularly well represented (especially in Chaplin's comedy), even if copulation, dismemberment and defecation are exceedingly rare pleasures in the genre.

The two poles offered by Bakhtin should serve as *orientation* for a consideration of the body in comedy, rather than an either/or model to simply apply to the genre. The same is true of the other paradigms considered in this section. Each offered a general theory or a set of fairly broad observations that might be useful for advancing our sense

Buster and his girl: Buster Keaton and Margaret Leahy (publicity still).

of how the comic body might appear. But my aim in this project is not to come up with a broad theory or an overly generalized account of the comic body in such a diverse genre as Hollywood slapstick. Instead I want to refine our understanding of the genre by remaining sensitive to the *detail* of particular instances, and to the *variety* of ways in which the body is presented. For this reason I turn now to consider briefly some notable critical accounts of the genre.

The Body in Words: Some Critical Accounts of the Genre

A principal task of film criticism is to deepen an appreciation of its immediate object by finding just the right words to describe its exemplary qualities, and to elucidate how such qualities are significant. As Stanley Cavell writes,

> ... the question what becomes of objects when they are filmed and screened — like the question what becomes of particular people, and specific locales, and subjects and motifs when they are filmed by individual makers of film — has only one source of data for its answer, namely the appearance and significance of just those objects and people that are in fact to be found in the succession of films, or passages of films, that matter to us. To express their appearances, and define those significances, and articulate the nature of this mattering, are acts that help to constitute what we might call film criticism.[20]

Accordingly, the only "source of data" for an answer to the question of "what becomes of the body on film?" (at least, in the Hollywood film genre of slapstick comedy) is precisely the "appearance and significance" of the body in the passages of films that strike me as exemplary instances of the genre. My undertaking, therefore, is to "express [these] appearances" and "define those significances" by means of a form of writing that attends to the detail and meaning of such instances.

It may seem surprising, given the centrality of the body in movie slapstick, that few writers have attended, in any detail and depth, to the *physical* aspect of physical comedy. Nonetheless, some notable contributions to the field of film criticism on this genre have been formative in encouraging my investigations into this topic. Alan Dale writes that "slapstick doesn't *say* anything about our condition as physical beings, though that is its one great subject,"[21] but a sustained analysis of *how* this "one great subject" is explored or invoked strangely does not feature in Dale's useful and often perceptive book-length account of slapstick in American movies. Similarly, Gerald Mast announces that "the great silent comedies revolve about the body and the personality of its owner," but while his book illustrates how the films of the great silent comedians constitute a "comedy of personality," Mast doesn't fully justify the former part of the claim by showing how, and to what effect, the body occupies such a position of centrality.[22] Mast's understanding of the genre casts quite a sharp line between silent and sound comedy, as well as between the body and the mind, claiming that "whereas the silent performer was a physical being — and only through the physical an intellectual one — the sound performer was both physical and intellectual at once."[23] Indeed, for Mast, the body ceases to be a central subject for sound comedy,[24] a notion I set out to investigate in Chapter 6, entitled "Body and Voice."

Frank Krutnik has surveyed the presentation of the body in the comedy of Jerry Lewis, claiming that Lewis "parades a spectacle of the body in disruption, a body that is othered from the self," in which "grotesque convulsions fragment bodily expression into a collage of misdirected and disconnected gestures."[25] Krutnik's hyperbolic style (of which this quotation is quite representative) is no doubt in part an attempt to counter forcefully the tendency of film critics to dismiss Lewis as crude or uninteresting. As a consequence, however, Krutnik's claims tend towards the grandiose and generalized, and because they are rarely supported by specific reference, they often lack in precision. For instance, Krutnik declares in his Introduction that Lewis offers "an extreme form of physical comedy in which the unruly body *overturns its subjugation* to the intellect, to the spirit, to speech ... [and one which] presents the spectacle of a body *liberated* ... from social and physical constraints."[26] Later on, however, Krutnik agrees with Steven Shaviro[27] that Lewis replaces "the cathartic structure expected from physical comedy with the *discomfiting* presentation

Stella Stevens with Jerry Lewis as Professor Julius Kelp in *The Nutty Professor* (1963)

of a body *writhing in subjugation.*"[28] Since both are presented as general statements designed to characterize Lewis's comedy, the unacknowledged contradiction between these two claims — between a 'liberating' and 'discomfiting' effect, and between a body "overturn[ing]" and "writhing in" subjugation — is something of a source of confusion. It is not especially fanciful to believe that Lewis's comedy might at turns present the body as "liberated ... from social and physical constraints" (although not *all* social and physical constraints, surely?) and in other sequences present the body as "writhing in subjugation." But the generalized nature of the claims, together with the imprecise use of the word "subjugation" and the lack of detailed support, make them seem mutually competitive (rather than representing, say, a claim for the range of Lewis's work). The example should alert us to the need for substantial claims to arise out of descriptive analysis, so that interpretations are verifiable, being based on observable detail.

Walter Kerr, by contrast, in his outstanding contribution to the literature on silent physical comedy, rarely strays far from the detail of particular moments, and as a result his characterizations of the figures of Chaplin, Keaton, Harold Lloyd and Harry Langdon are often insightful and nuanced. By working through specific examples at a rapid but never dismissive pace, Kerr sketches, with some authority, how each major film comedian of the silent era developed a distinctive style of comedy. Often this takes the form of working through the logic of gags by describing with care how the moment unravels. Here is Kerr on Chaplin's use of visual metaphor:

> There is a justly celebrated sequence in *The Pawnshop* [1916] — composed of the two longest sustained "takes" Chaplin had yet permitted himself — in which he is asked by a customer to examine a clock. What will Charlie give him for it? Charlie must test the reliability of the clock. He applies a stethoscope to it, turning it into a sick baby. Failing to get to its insides with an auger, he turns it into a can of tuna fish and cuts away its lid with an opener. It does not have a very hopeful odor. The insides are attacked with a jeweler's eyeglass; it is delicate Swiss-work now. But its teeth are bad and a dentist's forceps must be applied. Defective plumbing too: a hammer will help. Its inner mechanisms begin to uncoil. He measures and snips them off like yardgoods. When its minor parts begin to squiggle about on the counter like larvae, he uses an oil can as exterminator. He gathers the parts together into

the man's hat and gives them back. No deal. A clock—unlikely object—can be a baby, a can of fish, an open mouth, a bolt of cotton—*anything*. Chaplin has gone beyond mere look-alikes. The identity of an object lies only in the attitude one takes toward it. The man of all attitudes makes the universe his helpless plaything.[29]

Kerr's description of the sequence captures the logic and development of the sequence by evoking a moment-by-moment experience of it, so that his description forms a certain kind of analysis *in itself.* We might notice, for instance, how the claim that "Chaplin has gone beyond mere look-alikes" has already been reflected in the manner of description, which starts by highlighting Chaplin's role in actively transforming the clock ("turning it into" a sick baby, and then into a can of tuna fish) and then eliminates even this intervention when the clock suddenly 'becomes' an open mouth ("its teeth are bad..."), as if the object were actually morphing before our eyes. In fact, the description manages to be evocative without even mentioning the shifting stance of Charlie's body behind the desk, the detail of his gestures, or his ever-changing facial expressions. While a trace of such features remains in the way Kerr captures Charlie's shifting *attitude* to the object (so "it does not have a very hopeful odor" replaces the need to describe Charlie's impish sniffing of the clock, and his subsequent expression of disgust), the physical detail of the moment is not brought out directly. Such an approach may be perfectly apposite here for an account of the scene that wishes to suggest the way visual metaphor attempts a disavowal of the literal, physical status of the objects presented to our view. But an exploration of the physicality of performance, of the deployment and presentation of the body, is not a key feature of Kerr's analysis, here or elsewhere.

In his justly celebrated article, "Comedy's Greatest Era," James Agee's nostalgia for the silent clowns does not detract from the sharpness of his insights. In the format of a short article (originally published in *Life* magazine in 1949) that sought to recall with fondness the great days of silent film comedy, it is unsurprising that Agee finds little space to analyze the physical detail of particular moments. Yet his characterizations of figures from silent slapstick evoke their appearance

Buster Keaton, accelerating towards a "flogged-piston sprint."

with such precision that they help us see those figures more clearly than we could before. Consider, for example, Agee's impressionistic description of slapstick bit player Mack Swain, "who looked like a hairy mushroom, rolling his eyes in a manner patented by the French romantics and gasping in some dubious ecstasy"; or his remarkable sketch of "snouty" James Finlayson (best known from Laurel and Hardy films), "gleefully foreclosing a mortgage, with his look of eternally tasting a spoiled pickle."[30] Most pertinently for this study, Agee's vivid description of Buster Keaton, framed as a general memory rather than referring to a specific instance, offers a valuable account of the performer's physical bearing:

> His short-legged body was all sudden, machine-like angles, governed by a daft aplomb. When he swept a semaphore-like arm to point, you could almost hear the electrical impulse in the signal block. When he ran from a cop his transitions from accelerating walk to easy jogtrot to brisk canter to headlong gallop to flogged-piston sprint — always floating, above this frenzy, the untroubled, untouchable face — were as distinct and as soberly in order as an automatic gearshift.

It is important to notice how Agee's description of Keaton's body-as-machine relents from falling into the realm of caricature. Instead, the mechanistic imagery is shaded by such touches as the oxymoronic "daft aplomb" (succinctly conveying the absurdity of

Keaton's composure and aptitude), and the reference to the face as "floating," which offers just the slightest hint of a ghostlike quality (the ghost in the machine, perhaps). This tension between the mechanistic and ethereal in Keaton's body is expressed in the contrast between the unbroken syntax conveying the speed and smoothness of his gearshifts ("brisk canter to headlong gallop to flogged-piston sprint") and the visionary description of Keaton's "untroubled, untouchable face," slowed by commas and held apart in dashes, itself floating free of the headlong rush of words — untouchable. In this way, Agee justifies the use of evocative description as a means of articulating a meaning-ful experience of film. At the same time, he demonstrates the worth of attending to the body as such, in a genre that invites us to experience the physicality of the world anew.

1

Body and Mind:
Charlie Chaplin

This chapter will contend that the comedy of Charlie Chaplin, particularly his short films made for Mutual in 1916–17, can be seen to invoke and manifest relations between body and mind. In several respects these films can be seen to present a sort of caricature or parody of Cartesian philosophy, playing on the idea of a mind/body distinction and on the related conception of the body as a machine-like object. My claim here is not that Chaplin set out to explore philosophical ideas; it is more likely that an intuitive grasp of what might produce a certain kind of comic effect led him towards such a strategy. What I am calling Chaplin's parody of Cartesian philosophy is all the more effective because in powerful ways his films offer a vivid sense of the *unity* of body and mind. While the ontology of the silent film is already such that we grasp the mind *through* the body (rather than, as in literature, through description), few performers have achieved such lucidity of expression as Charlie Chaplin, and so few performers have so strikingly created the impression of the mind as perfectly *visible*. Stanley Cavell has written of "the sublime comprehensibility of Chaplin's natural choreography,"[1] evoking the spectacle of apparent effortlessness with which Chaplin manifests thoughts and feelings in the motions and behavior of his body. This observation in turn bears resemblance to a claim made for film more generally by the philosopher

Maurice Merleau-Ponty, who could have asked for no better case in point than Chaplin:

> ... This is why the movies can be so gripping in their presentation of man: they do not give us his thoughts, as novels have done for so long, but his conduct or behavior. [...] For the movies, as for modern psychology, dizziness, pleasure, grief, love, and hate are ways of behaving. [...] The movies are peculiarly suited to make manifest the union of mind and body ... and the expression of one in the other.[2]

According to Merleau-Ponty, the presentation of human behavior in the movies serves to dissolve (before our eyes, so to speak) any conceptual distinction between mind and body. In the Cartesian model, feelings such as pleasure or grief are immaterial and thus invisible states of mind that are known only to the first person. Such feelings may be betrayed by outward, involuntary bodily signs such as smiling or crying, and from these signs an observer might be able to venture an interpretation as to what that person is feeling. Merleau-Ponty, however, rejects such a model:

> We must reject that prejudice which makes "inner realities" out of love, hate, or anger, leaving them accessible to one single witness: the person who feels them. Anger, shame, hate, and love are not psychic facts hidden at the bottom of another's consciousness: they are types of behavior or styles of conduct which are visible from the outside ... we cannot say that only the signs of love or anger are given to the outside observer and that we understand others indirectly by interpreting these signs: we have to say that others are directly manifest to us as behavior.[3]

The dichotomy of inner/mind and outer/body is refuted by an understanding of anger as a form of behavior, rather than an intangible psychic condition. It makes no sense to think of behavior as a bodily referent to the hidden mental state of "anger." For Merleau-Ponty, the behavior of anger *is* anger, and as such anger is directly perceptible. Film's special capacity to make behavior visible, thus to show thoughts and feelings directly, is therefore understood by Merleau-Ponty to collapse the Cartesian dichotomy between unthinking corporeality and the immaterial mind.

Consider, for example, *The Adventurer* (1917), in which Chaplin plays an escaped convict posing as an aristocrat amidst a party of gen-

1. Body and Mind: Charlie Chaplin

The unmistakable expression of someone who has just dropped a lump of ice cream down his pants: Charlie Chaplin in *The Adventurer* (1917).

teel socialites. When Charlie and the girl are served ice cream on the mansion balcony, the demands of urbane manners, together with the desire to present himself as a sophisticated bachelor in order to woo the girl, oblige a containment of his bodily response: firstly, to the tingle of ice cream on the nerves of his untutored teeth, and then, when the bulk of it slips off the spoon, to the biting chill of an icy lump sliding down the front of his oversized trousers. Here, the very restraint in his reaction — a tenseness in the jaw, a little side-glance to camera, the mounting agitation in his eyes, a series of squirms disguised as discreet fidgets — directly conveys both his discomfort and anxiety. An uncouth reaction to the ice cream would upset his chances with the girl and ruin his hopes of avoiding detection; so to indulge his desires he must dampen his urges, and to remain a free man he must restrain his impulses. We can see a train of possible solutions running frantically through his mind. The utter expressiveness of Chaplin's performance, captured in a series of privileged views, offers the impression of complete transparency. Hence we are privy not merely to the responses of his body or to the fluctuations of his mind, but to their *synthesis* in the form of behavior.

Another example of this synthesis can be found in Chaplin's entrance as a languid waiter in *The Rink* (1916). Trudging from the kitchen, rounding the corner with a tired lilt, arms drooped at his sides, a napkin dangling from his hand like a rag: his weary apathy is *directly* apparent in the very attitude of his body. A corpulent bourgeois customer beckons him over for the bill; Charlie performs an insolent mock-salute and waddles over to the table, tucking the napkin under his armpit and slouching beside the customer, hand on hip. In a situation where he is expected to conceal such feelings, Charlie's disdain for the customer is not cloaked, but perfectly and precisely *visible*. The film's undemonstrative presentation of the action, while helping to evoke the waiter's lethargic disregard, importantly allows Chaplin's body to become the most meaningful element of the scene. Rather than, for instance, presenting a series of

Chaplin as a waiter in *The Rink* (1916).

close-ups of each detail of his appearance (the traipsing feet, the arms, the napkin), the film permits us to apprehend Charlie's state of mind without recourse to a series of delineated signs. Body and mind speak in one voice, an expressive whole.

The same is true of the bourgeois customer, whose sense of innate superiority is immediately captured in the way he slumps in his chair, brashly summons Charlie over, and turns back again to pick out some food from between his teeth. Yet Charlie's treat-

30

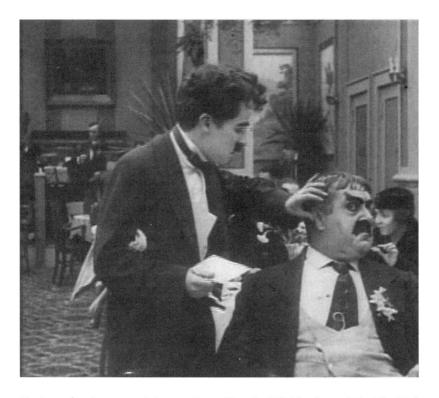

**Vestiges of melon around the ear: Compiling the bill Charlie-style in *The Rink*
(1916).**

ment of the customer is audaciously impertinent. Pulling out a notepad
to compile the bill, he scans over the customer's bulging torso and writes
down the contents of the order by piecing together the remnants of food-
stuff spilled down his front and more generally about his person: specks
of soup spattered on his shirt; a stray strand of spaghetti on his tie; vestiges of melon around the ear. The manner is humorously matter-of-fact:
he doesn't *ask* the customer what he ate; not only would Charlie not trust
his word, but he takes it for granted that this fellow is enough of a slob
as to have spilled a bit of everything somewhere. His offhand inspection
turns the customer's body into an object of scrutiny, as he fingers the sides
of the head to examine the hairline with mild disinterest. In this way, the
compiling of the bill resembles a coroner's analysis, with the customer as

the corpulent corpse around which various clues are liberally scattered. By disregarding the customer's subjectivity entirely, this unabashed examination (mirroring to some extent the conditions of viewing in the cinema, where the viewer is not compelled to respect the personal space or integrity of figures onscreen) enacts a kind of Cartesian dissection, a severance of mind from body. The body is understood to constitute an index of what lies within, but the only form of interiority of interest to Charlie is what may be swilling around in the customer's guts.

Charlie's callous transmutation of bodies into mere objects is by no means uncharacteristic of his early short films (and his impish cruelty should serve as a counterpoise for those who like to emphasize Chaplin's sentimentality). Walter Kerr evocatively captures this roguish behavior in his account of Chaplin's early style of performance:

> Having knocked someone down, he promptly used him as a doormat. Wanting a kiss from a girl, he seized her nose with dental pliers and drew her to him. He tossed his own baby about as though it were a rag doll, pushed his wife in the face and tumbled her over.[4]

As Kerr's description emphasizes, Chaplin's capacity to transform one thing into another, merely through his behavioral attitude towards it, stretches to include people as well. It comes as a result of his directing his behavior towards only the *physical* aspect of the person, and may remind us of Henri Bergson's contention that "we laugh every time a person gives us the impression of being a thing."[5] For instance, in his Essanay film *A Night at the Show* (1915), Chaplin plays a well-to-do drunkard making a pest of himself during a performance at a music hall. Taking a seat on the front row and awaiting the show with a contemptuous sneer while the musicians tune up in the adjacent pit, Charlie pulls out a match, strikes it on the bald head of a tuba player, and lights a cigarette. There has rarely been a more succinct encapsulation of the idea of utilitarian bourgeois consumption. The tuba player is there to serve a purpose, and that is to accommodate the paying punter in every conceivable way. The skill and sensibility of the musician are irrelevant to Charlie at the present moment. The only property of any import is the latent friction of a convenient bald head: rubbery skin stretched tightly enough over a hard cranium so as to enable the lighting of a match.

1. Body and Mind: Charlie Chaplin

Charlie Chaplin strikes up the band in *A Night at the Show* (1915).

The essential distinction between a person and a mere object — that the former may possess thoughts and feelings, while the latter is literally mindless — is crucially refused by Charlie in this moment of callous insensitivity. But the gesture also calls to our attention the "thingness" of people, declaring in its brashness the fact that people *are* objects, physical things in the world, like matches and tubas and doormats. Indeed, gags in Chaplin's films quite often turn on the fact that people and objects share the same condition of physicality, and that the dominance of one over the other is not automatically assured. In *One A.M.* (1916), Charlie arrives home from a drunken evening to find himself assailed by a house full of hostile objects. His Odyssean journey to get some rest finds Charlie vying with doors, tables, rugs and beds, each of which refuse to submit to his ascendancy. A stuffed lynx and a tiger-skin rug menace him from both sides. A lurching clock-pendulum tumbles him backwards down the stairs. In a state

33

of drunken stupor, Charlie finds himself unable to assert his dominion over his everyday possessions, which seem to have taken on, in
the absence of his own powers of reason, a cunning and malicious
intent.

Stanley Cavell has linked Chaplin's relationships with objects
to a condition of the medium that he calls "ontological equality," deriving from the fact that "photographs are of the world, in which human
beings are not ontologically favored over the rest of nature, in which
objects are not props but natural allies (or enemies) of the human
character."[6] The camera does not, in itself, distinguish between objects
and people; both are subject to the same surface scrutiny; in effect,
the camera proposes an equivalence. The drunkard's vision of malev-
olent objects in *One A.M.*, the rendering of the tuba player's bald head
as an object in *A Night at the Show*, and the waiter's disinterested examination of the customer in *The Rink*: all suggest that Charlie shares
something of the camera's propensity to flatten out the distinction
between people and (other) objects. This may explain why, working
in a film studio in *Behind the Screen* (1916) and preparing a scene
for shooting, Charlie massages the scalp of a bearskin rug as if it
were a pampered actor. Since the camera's objective vision draws
no distinction between people and objects, why shouldn't the rug
deserve the movie star treatment? In particular, gags in the Mutual
films recurrently draw parallels between bodies and machines in a manner that might be thought to evoke and parody the Cartesian conception of the body as a machine. Mechanical seizures, reflex responses
and involuntary motions all offer the impression of the body as distinct from the intentional activities of the mind. Descartes' conception
of the body as operating beyond intention is succinctly captured when
he writes that:

> ... all the movements that we make without our will contributing thereto
> (as frequently happens when we breathe, walk, eat, and in fact perform all
> those actions which are common to us and to the brutes), only depend on
> the conformation of our members, and on the course which the spirits,
> excited by the heat of the heart, follow naturally in the brain, nerves, and
> muscles, just as the movements of a watch are produced simply by the
> strength of the springs and the form of the wheels.[7]

1. Body and Mind: Charlie Chaplin

This image of the body as a mechanical thing such as a watch finds parodic echo in Chaplin's gags. In *The Pawnshop* (1916), Charlie applies a stethoscope to an alarm clock and listens for the pulse produced by the strength of the springs and the form of the wheels. In *The Fireman* (1916), Charlie finds a crick in his neck and promptly uses an oil-can to lubricate the offending zone. In *Behind the Screen*, Charlie is assigned by the film director to manage the large lever controlling a stage trap-door; finding the lever a bit stiff to haul, Charlie oils the mechanism and then, in case the fault lies with him, oils his own elbow for good measure. The conception of the body as a machine encourages an understanding of "the will" as something distinct from the mechanical corpse it might occupy. Charlie's gestures of self-oiling thereby offer a caricature of the Cartesian paradigm by depicting a split between an intentional self (he who oils) and a machine-like body (that which is oiled).

In the passage quoted above, Descartes refers to eating as an example of an action which is merely bodily, occurring without the involvement of "the will," and thus permitting the notion of the human body as a thoughtless machine (a notion that, in turn, reifies the division between body and mind). The sequence in *Modern Times* (1936) in which Charlie is strapped to the feeding machine, stripped of his will and forced to endure a barrage of food, from soup to nuts, demonstrates how de-humanizing such a conception of the individual person can be, wherein the digestive system of human beings is thought to constitute a kind of internal assembly line. Nevertheless, Chaplin's preoccupation with the pangs of hunger and the processes of eating can be found to relate to a comic idea that the body is a sort of machine, chiming with Bergson's discovery of a source of laughter in the appearance of "something mechanical encrusted on the living."[8] In *Behind the Screen*, Charlie stares in awe at the pile of pies comprising his enormous workmate's lunch, measuring the fellow's mammoth gut before giving him the all-clear, and we have already seen how the scattered remnants of the customer's meal in *The Rink* provide evidence of the mechanistic procedure of chewing and slurping, spilling and digesting, rationalizing Charlie's impersonal treatment towards this guzzling-machine of a man.

The Body in Hollywood Slapstick

Suggestions of the mechanistic body are set alongside the fluidity that characterizes Chaplin's performance. The inert, lumpish body of the customer at the start of *The Rink* is juxtaposed against the swift ingenuity of Charlie's behavior, and, most strikingly, with his later exhibition of skating on the rink itself, a dazzling display of virtuosity. Chaplin's skating, like Fred Astaire's dancing, seems to gather momentum without propulsion. An almost excessive grace, accentuated by balletic hand and arm gestures together with a breezily casual posture, forms the subject of humor as we see him glide out of the changing area and onto the rink for the first time. Seconds earlier, in the foyer, he had seemed rather clumsy as he tottered on his roller skates and fell into the laps of two young ladies waiting on a bench, but now his subsequent proficiency exposes the ruse behind this "accident." It so happens that the portly customer from the restaurant is also skating on the rink this afternoon, and after performing some teasing circles around this unsteady novice, Charlie glides in an arc with an outstretched leg, acknowledging an appreciative crowd around the rink. The camera loosely follows his trajectory, until, out of nowhere, it seems, Charlie abruptly crashes foot-first into his rival, much to the mirth of the assembled crowd. This intentional accident is followed by a bout of involuntary taunting. With the large man in a heap on the floor, Charlie undertakes to get to his feet, but appears to find them suddenly unsteady. Apparently struggling to find his balance, Charlie's legs become a blur of movement, as each foot in turn with lightning-speed takes the place of the retracting foot to bear the weight of his floundering body. Lurching violently forward as if about to collapse head-first onto his flinching rival, Charlie's flurry of reflex activity seems at once deliberate *and* inadvertent.

Chaplin's comedy frequently dramatizes the ambiguity of intention, playing on the blurred line between calculated and spontaneous, premeditative and circumstantial, involuntary and purposeful behavior. Such a depiction resembles Merleau-Ponty's contention that "psychological motives and bodily occasions may overlap because there is not a single impulse in a living body which is entirely fortuitous in relation to psychic intentions, not a single mental act which has not at

A deliberate accident? Charlie Chaplin and Eric Campbell in *The Rink* (1916).

least its germ or its general outline in physiological tendencies."[9] In the above instance from *The Rink*, both the original collision and Charlie's frantic floundering seem "not entirely fortuitous in relation to psychic intentions," yet still appear unpremeditated, a corollary of circumstance, inclination and reflex. Such an impression flouts the Cartesian conception of an unthinking body conjoined to an intentional mind. Instead, intention springs from both body *and* mind.

The appearance of virtuosity, such as we apprehend in Chaplin's graceful skating, presents a perfect harmony between body and mind, an intertwining of mental and physical proficiency. Such deftness renders it impossible to conceive of the mind-body relation as that between, say, operator and machine. Conversely, a marked loss of control can imply a certain distance between mind and body by foregrounding a palpable distinction between intention and execution. Chaplin's comedy is notable for a fluid movement between these two

Pride comes before a fall: Charlie shows off for Edna Purviance in _The Vagabond_ (1916).

extremes. In _The Vagabond_ (1916), Charlie is a wandering fiddler who endeavors to impress a gypsy girl with his musical talent. His artful poise assures us of his virtuosity as he bows the violin with smooth, elegant strokes. Enchanted by the beautiful sounds she hears emanating from the fiddle, the girl awakens from her servitude to the washboard and gazes longingly into space. Having secured her pliancy, Charlie then launches into a vigorous, rhythmic attack on the strings, sending the girl into mechanical convulsions, before returning to the romantic air with which he began. Charlie's remote control over the girl's body is flaunted in the gestural flourish of swiftly running the bow along under his nose and raising his eyebrows, maestro-style. This cheeky nose-wipe declares a mastery of his own body as of the violin, a mastery that has temporarily uncoupled the girl's body from her mind.

Yet as he launches once again into a forceful musical assault, his mind overcome with artistic passions, his body jitters backwards and tumbles into a large tub of water.

A pratfall such as this seems to set mind and body at variance. At the start of *Easy Street* (1917), Charlie leaves a local church service with a sense of spiritual redemption; he even hands back to the pastor the collection box that he had formerly stuffed down his pants. He exits with his hands clasped before him and his head held high, gazing towards the heavens. Yet Charlie's newly obtained faith in the future has left him blind to what lies ahead of him. No sooner has he set forth from the door than he indecorously stumbles down the chapel steps, in a manner most out of keeping with a newfound sense of grace. Charlie's mind was in the clouds, forgetting his feet were still touching the ground. On the constantly rolling deck of the ship in *The Immigrant*

Charlie Chaplin in *The Immigrant* (1916). Next to him in the front row are Edna Purviance (center) and Kitty Bradbury.

(1916), Charlie is smitten with a young lady and offers her his seat in the dining cabin. As he goes to leave, he stops at the door to gaze at her for a moment, tenderly, sweetly, as she ties up the knot of her head-scarf. Then all at once the lurching of the ship catches up with him: his lovesick grin evaporates into a spasm of retching, and he hastens outside to vomit. Each of these moments involves an apparent disjuncture between mind and body, in which the former is interrupted, as it were, by the latter. In *Easy Street*, Charlie's spiritual uplift is dislodged by a stumble down the stairs. In *The Immigrant*, Charlie's feelings of love are momentarily set aside by a sudden requirement to throw up. Each moment hinges on a comic sense of the body as detached from emotional states, indifferent to the feelings of its owner.

The Immigrant works in other ways to imply a detachment between body and mind. Indeed, the film repeatedly foregrounds the fact that true feelings, thoughts, intentions, and so on, are often far from visible to the observer. The captain's mistaken assumption that Charlie intends to steal from the girl (when actually he was in the process of putting his gambling winnings into her pocket), and the artist's later misapprehension in the restaurant that Charlie genuinely doesn't want him to pay the bill (when, in fact, without a penny to his name, Charlie was just overdoing gestures of polite refusal), provide two such instances of the mind being comically hidden from view. Indeed, out first view of Charlie in the film involves a sight gag that plays on the fact that the body can mislead. Draped over the edge of the ship and rhythmically convulsing, it appears for all the world that Charlie is throwing up overboard. Yet he suddenly pulls himself back onto deck and turns around to face the camera with a cheeky grin, a makeshift fishing line in one hand and a freshly-caught fish in the other. The moment involves the spectator in a realization that appearances can be deceptive. An apparently passive body, juddering with spasms, turned out to be actively deployed, the spasms revealed to be intentional motions directed towards the catching of a fish. The structure of the gag is replayed in a later film, *The Idle Class* (1921), in which Chaplin plays an aristocrat who has been left by his wife on account of his excessive drinking. Having just read the "Dear John" letter, the

Shaken, not stirred: Chaplin prepares a consolatory cocktail in *The Idle Class* (1921).

aristocrat turns slowly away from the camera and his body is overcome with sob-like shakes. It is only when he turns back around again that we realize that he has been fixing himself a cocktail. The motions we observed were taken as signs of inconsolable anguish, yet they proved to signify nothing more than the vigorous mixing of drinks in a shaker. Of course, this is not to deny that the aristocrat may still be feeling heartbroken; the shaking of cocktails may well result from grief as much as from nonchalance. But his body here is resolutely undemonstrative of emotion, the index of a crippling reticence that lies at the core of his troubles.

Working against the grain of film's capacity to reveal, the moment conveys the obscurity of feelings, just as *The Immigrant* suggests the hiddenness of intentions. While the mind may become manifest, as Merleau-Ponty wishes to emphasize, in the revelatory motions of behavior, thoughts and feelings may equally remain cloaked from view. What the body shows does not always reveal; film is just as well placed to play upon the ambiguity of mental states as upon their transparency. While Merleau-Ponty's claims for film rest upon an assumption of the expressiveness and indeed honesty of the body, these two sight gags depend upon the capacity of the body to mislead us in our reading of characters' states of mind. With one hand, Chaplin solicits our trust in posture and gesture to perfectly manifest states of mind; with the other, he lampoons our blind faith in this connection.

Even Charlie, it seems, can be duped in this regard. Working behind the counter in *The Pawnshop*, Charlie is approached by a desperate customer bewailing the loss of his dear wife and forced, by a financial misfortune, to pawn her cherished wedding ring, the one item he has left in the world to remind him of her. At first, as the old man relates his sad story, gazing upwards and treading pensively, hands held in agony, Charlie cynically chews on his apple and pulls out a mallet from behind the till: this guy looks like a right one. Demonstratively continuing his sad story, the old man places one hand inside his coat

Fooled by the body: Charlie begins to melt in *The Pawnshop* (1916).

and the other arm behind his straight back: a dignitary down on his luck, but still proud. Charlie grabs an antique camera from the shelf behind him and cheekily snaps this old-timer for posterity: a fitting subject for the camera. Gradually, however, as the old man sobbingly tells his tale — head shaking, hand on heart, arms gesturing to the heavens — Charlie begins to melt, choking on his apple in a series of spluttery sobs. Entirely won over by the story, and wiping a tear from his eye, he values the ring at five dollars, offers the old man ten, and gives him the ring back as well.

It is only when the old man reaches into his pocket to add it to a huge stack of bills that Charlie realizes he has been swindled. He blinks in disbelief, grins insanely at the camera and knocks *himself* over the head with the mallet. Gesticulations of the body can seem so convincingly expressive of true emotion that they can fool even the most cynical observer. Charlie's gesture of hitting himself on the head with the hammer — an acknowledgement of his suckerdom — rhymes with a later moment when, eager to get rid of yet another irksome customer, Charlie smacks him with another hammer, from which the customer dizzily recoils. Then, in a curiously reflexive gesture, Charlie twangs the hammer-head to reveal the tool to be made of rubber — an acknowledgement of the film's artifice, so perhaps of our own suckerdom. How else are we to understand the customer's dizzy reaction to a rubber hammer except by the fact that he is an actor in Chaplin's film, no less a pretender than the old quack with the wedding ring? Merleau-Ponty asserts that film can manifest a mind-body union by virtue that "for the movies ... dizziness [and] grief ... are ways of behaving." But as *The Pawnshop* makes evident, dizziness and grief can also be ways of *performing.*

Merleau-Ponty perhaps overlooks the fact that figures in a fiction film are ontologically dualistic: they are not just characters, transparently "behaving," but actors too, masking their own immediate thoughts and feelings in going through the motions of a role. In some ways, the relationship between performer and character can be thought to parallel the relationship between mind and body, and even to produce an effect of their unity or distinction. In the transparent presen-

43

tation of behavior, character and performer can seem so thoroughly intertwined that there is no sense of a distinction between the two. At other times, a split is more pronounced. The moments detailed above from *The Pawnshop*, *The Idle Class* and *The Immigrant* each draw upon and heighten our awareness that characters are being performed by acknowledging, in the former, that objects are mere props in a slapstick routine, or, in the latter two, that actions have been arranged to be viewed from a specific angle for an intentional comic effect. Part of an appreciation of such gags entails a recognition that certain mental processes have been *deliberately* obscured by the performer.

Similarly, when Charlie tumbles backwards into a tub of water in *The Vagabond*, the spontaneous roll of applause that might accompany this moment in a screening points to our awareness that such an action has been *intentionally* performed for our pleasure. A pratfall such as this one thus manufactures a split between the falling body of Charlie — who has inadvertently tumbled against his will — and the intending entity of Chaplin — who meant to do it. In this sense, such moments might be thought to recall the Cartesian dichotomy between body and mind which is similarly split along intentional lines (between the body without a will and the intentional entity of the mind). The dual presence of performer and character may imply a fundamental dualism in the figures onscreen in a fiction film.

Such moments can equally be thought to complicate a clean distinction between the intentional and the unintentional. That Chaplin's character is frequently a performer himself, as he is in the moment from *The Vagabond*, performing for audiences *within* the film, is one such area of complication (is the fall in fact an intended part of *Charlie's* performance?). Moreover, our more or less latent knowledge that characters are being performed means that we are inclined to attribute a degree of intention to even the most evidently unintentional bodily movements, such as falling backwards into a bucket. Our awareness that a pratfall contains a trace of intention — that it is a deliberate accident — is a crucial part of its effect (and goes some way to explain why we are perhaps more likely to laugh at somebody falling over on the screen than on the street). Chaplin is particularly sophisticated in his manipulation of such an awareness. The very cheekiness of Charlie, for example — perhaps his most defining characteristic — depends upon at least a whisper of intention in everything he does, together with the fact that everything he does is, in some sense, revelatory of a particular state of mind. Chaplin's comedy thus declares and draws to its advantage two momentous conditions of the fiction film: firstly, the condition of actor-character coexistence which posits a trace of intention in every bodily movement but implies a fundamental dualism; and secondly, the condition of visibility that can manifest thoughts and feelings directly in behavior.

Chaplin's comedy oscillates between an impression of mind and body as a cohesive whole, and an impression of mind and body as distinct and disparate. Indeed, the co-incidence of these mutually conflicting impressions generates a prevailing sense of comic incongruity. The Cartesian notion of a fundamental distinction between the physical body and the immaterial mind continues to exert some force over our everyday conceptions of ourselves and others, despite the efforts of many philosophers to shake us free of this impression. Our sense of the separateness of body and mind may be prompted by the frequent difficulties faced in determining what others are *really* thinking or feeling: if the body is misleading, then the mind remains hidden, elusive, intangible. The impression of the body as a machine-like object, acting of its own volition, outside of our control (an impression that powerfully comes to the fore during periods of illness, for example), further compounds the idea that mind and body are distinct and disparate entities. It is difficult to reconcile such impressions with the conflicting notion that mind and body comprise a unified whole. As Descartes himself declares:

> It does not seem to me that the human mind is capable of conceiving very distinctly, and at the same time, both the distinction between mind and body, and their union. To do that, it is necessary to consider them as a single thing and at the same time consider them as two things, which is self-contradictory.[10]

Chaplin's comedy asks us to do just that.

2

Body and World:
Buster Keaton

Keaton's world is a large world. His slight frame is consistently set against the bulky builds of urban bullies, dwarfed beside giant machines and other outsized objects, within extensive landscapes whose sparse, uncluttered planes stretch laterally across the screen and in depth to the distant horizon. In addition, the cultivation of a strong sense of expansive offscreen space — through editing across a range of broad terrains and by gags based on what cannot be seen on account of the camera's cropping[1] — works to suggest a world larger, more full of possibility and hazard, than any single person could conceivably survey or account for. We need only think of the deserted ocean liner in *The Navigator* (1924), itself adrift in a vast grey sea, to consider how the largeness of Keaton's environments is used to expressive effect through its relation to the diminutive body. At one point in that film, Keaton's hero tries to tug the huge drifting vessel using only a one-man rowing boat, the vanity of his endeavors demonstrated by a cut to extreme long shot, parallel to the length of the ship, in which his figure is barely a speck on the desolate landscape. The futility of human determination has already been hinted at in the earlier scene in which Keaton and his girl repeatedly fail to find one another aboard the vessel; here, too, the camera withdraws to far-shot, likening their searching motions to the intricate activity of a mechanical toy as they race around the

46

decks. In reducing through scale the body to a figure, and placing it within a vast impersonal locale composed with geometrical precision, Keaton's comedy is tinged with a certain fascinating coldness that is not found, for instance, in Chaplin's rendering of body-world relations.

Keaton's regular employment of the far-shot, particularly in his early two-reelers,[2] is just one way in which he places emphasis on the movement of figures in space over, say, the social or psychological facets of behavior that acquire greater stress in Chaplin's comedy. We might say that while Chaplin primarily discovers comic significance in the body's relation to character and to society at large, Keaton discovers it primarily in the body's relation to space and motion. Consider, for example, two ostensibly similar opening sequences from contemporaneous Chaplin and Keaton films in which the central figure arrives by train. In Chaplin's *The Idle Class* (1921), a train pulls into a station and several wealthy

Charlie Chaplin arrives by train in *The Idle Class* (1921).

Buster Keaton arrives by train in _The High Sign_ (1921).

types — monocled, pipe-smoking, each with a set of golf clubs — step
down from the First-Class carriage. Further down the length of the train,
the hefty flap to a luggage hold is kicked open by a pair of oversized boots,
and the Tramp emerges from the train's cramped underbelly. He dusts
himself down, magisterially stretches his legs and retrieves his _own_ golf
clubs from the hold. Made in the same year, Keaton's _The High Sign_ opens
with a train roaring past, close and across the frame at ninety degrees to
the camera, filling the screen with its left-to-right motion. Without fore-
warning, a figure is hurled from the passing vehicle into the sand below,
tumbling from screen-left and landing in a heap right in the middle of
the shot. As the figure climbs to his feet, we see it is Buster. His vertical body now bisects the frame, and as the tail-end of the train finally
passes a vast space ahead of him now opens up in depth, flanked by
buildings, all the way to the ocean horizon. Buster stands for a moment
with his back to us, glances left and right, and then wanders off screen-

48

right. Whereas Chaplin lays stress on the body's *social* placement within a scenario that draws contrasts and comparisons between rich and poor, Keaton lays stress on the body's *spatial* placement within a composition that takes delight in the contrast of movement and stillness, calculation and randomness, nearness and depth.

This feature is especially prominent in Keaton's short chase films made between 1920 and 1922.[3] Four of these two-reelers — *Cops* (1922) *Neighbors* (1921), *The Paleface* (1922) and *The Goat* (1921) — stand out as exemplary of Keaton's tendency towards abstract, spatial play between body and world. In *Cops*, Buster finds himself being hunted by a huge swarm of cops after having unwittingly disrupted the ordered formations of the Annual Policemen's Parade. The irony of his having been mistaken for an anarchist is afforded extra weight in the ensuing chase, when the compositional organization of trailing policemen

A swarm of policeman chases down Buster in *Cops* (1922). Notice the loosely geometrical composition formed by the archway and the triangle of trailing cops.

around Buster's solitary body constitutes a more impressive formal arrangement than the original parade. A particularly remarkable shot occurs about fifteen minutes into the film, when Buster hides inside the entrance of a building to avoid two bands of cops who surge past outside. We are not invited to share Buster's alarm at the sight of cops closing in on him; rather, we are invited to take pleasure in the neatness of his evasion, a pleasure permitted by the classical beauty of our privileged perspective that allows us to see the unity of apparently haphazard action. The camera is placed so that the door is precisely in the center of the frame and the perspective lines of two streets stretch away into the distance either side of that entrance. The striking symmetry of the framing is matched by an amusingly meticulous symmetry of movement: Buster darts right and then left before disappearing inside the central door; the two bands of cops appear simultaneously from left and right, crisscross directly outside the door before filing away down opposite streets; Buster enters the frame running from behind the camera's near left side, and exits the frame symmetrically running past the camera's near right side. The latter feature gives the shot a circular unity, and wittily declares Keaton's controlling hand as director in the way he resumes his place behind and beside the camera at the end of the take, as if just in time to yell "cut!" This figure's alignment with the camera is accordingly signaled in the visual configuration, which places the camera at the apex of one "V" that the cops rush down, and Keaton's body at the apex of another, inverted, V when he disappears inside the building. We are thus made strongly aware of a conditioning force behind the action we see and the images we watch. Racing into shot, Keaton's body takes its place in a world transfigured by the camera's view of it.

Keaton's reliance on location shooting is significant in this regard. The city locale of *Cops* is quite clearly a real city, not a painted studio backdrop. When Buster emerges hurtling from a dusty backalley, followed seconds later by a horde of cops, the framing of the image appears casual, almost haphazard, cropping the edge off street signs and parked cars, including quite a lot of foreground blank space, and with no special effort having been made to prettify the composition by removing

Symmetry as comedy: Buster temporarily evades his pursuers in *Cops* (1922).

the usual urban articles one would expect to find in a fairly run-down city district. Nevertheless, to our surprise, the shot achieves a formal beauty, primarily in the way Keaton's body operates in that space. Having sprinted the length of the alleyway to the road, Buster halts for just a second, turning towards his pursuers, before a car suddenly appears from the left and he latches on with one hand to be whisked away screen right. While his dash towards the camera emphasized the *depth* of the alleyway down which the camera looked directly, his sudden latching on to a passing car opens up a new perpendicular plane of movement, *across* the frame. The abrupt shift in angle is realized in Keaton's astonishing acrobatics, in the way his body is wrenched so forcefully away that his vertical figure becomes horizontal in flight. For such a stark formal arrangement to emerge from such an apparently casual set-up only adds to the moment's sense of pleasurable comic surprise. In playing unfussy photographic detail and a strict adherence

51

to the laws of physics against a more formal concern with movement, line and figure, Keaton blurs the boundary between physicality and abstraction.[4]

The city of *Cops* becomes increasingly abstracted as the film proceeds. In following Buster's efforts to become a successful businessman, the opening moments sketch a world of social contrasts — rich and poor, policemen and crooks — but the film's interest soon turns to less figurative contrasts of rhythm and scale. The sluggish speed of Buster's overstacked horse-and-cart, piled high with merchandise, is set at comic variance with the surrounding world of zippy automobiles and traffic cops; Buster's thoughtful pacing back and forth aboard the cart, humorously restricted by the vehicle's modest width, is contrasted with the large-scale pomp of the policemen's marching parade, filling the entire width of the concourse. By the time the chase breaks out and Keaton's solitary figure is pitted against the huge body of cops, surging like a wave after him, the city has become so fantasized that it no longer feels like a place of human inhabitance.

This partial abstraction of the world matches and expresses the sense of detachment between Keaton's hero and the workings of that world. We are offered the sense that this portrayal of the world corresponds to Buster's somewhat alien perspective, to his greater interest in physical properties than in the nuance of social interaction. To see the world as an intricate configuration of shape and movement is to see it at one remove. In *Neighbors*, this sense of disengagement is manifested in Buster's repeated attempts to view the world unseen.[5] At one point, Buster has hinged a plank above his backyard gate so that, when the gate is barged through at speed, the plank see-saws down and gives the barger a good whack on the backside. Having sufficiently antagonized his burly neighbor to burst through the gate and receive the first blow, Buster then climbs on top of the garden fence and watches this scene of escalating slapstick from behind some hanging laundry. As the neighbor sets about Buster's father whom he takes to be the culprit, some cops arrive to break up the dispute but they too become embroiled in the mayhem as they rush through the gate. One cop flies through a ground-floor window; another gets bashed on the head with the plank;

Buster retreats to view the world unseen: *Neighbors* (1921).

yet another trips over Buster's dizzy father. All the while, Buster watches intently from his vantage point behind the laundry. Yet despite the evident hilarity of the proceedings, he shows no sign of amusement. Instead, his facial expression remains one of rapt interest, as if he were studying the chains of cause and effect, the physical laws of momentum and equilibrium, the accumulation of misapprehension and mishap. In viewing, he temporarily ceases to be subject to these processes; his retreat to the position of viewing is suggestive not of a mischievous spirit but of a dream of being disembodied, where the neutrality of sitting on the fence exempts him from the world of action.

The fence has already been established as a motif associated with concealed viewing: in an early sequence, Buster's mother catches him peering through the fence to observe the reaction of the girl next-door to a note passed through a knothole; later, a cop catches Buster peeking through another fence to see Babe Ruth at bat, and just as Buster is being hauled away the ball flies over the fence and knocks the cop out cold. In both cases, the fence screens viewer from viewed, and yet both instances realize the possibility of the fence being penetrated or traversed (like the ghostly traversal of the cinema screen in *Sherlock Jr.* [1924]). The emphasis on the fence as dividing barrier is introduced in the composition of the film's opening shot — a high-angle far-shot showing Buster and the Girl leaning against the fence in their two respective adjacent backyards — by having the fence run precisely down the middle of the image. This bisection articulates the forbidden nature of their relationship but also implies, in its symmetry, a reciprocal balance between them (reiterated by their mutual passing of notes through the hole in the fence). Establishing the narrative problem of how these two lovebirds might be joined, the composition of this first image also suggests a solution, equally geometrical: above, and at a tangent to the strong vertical line of the fence, the washing lines stretch across the

Crossing boundaries: Buster slides the line in *Neighbors* (1921).

frame, spanning the two backyards in a visual suggestion of the possibility for cross-transference. The opportunity presents itself when the neighbors each side of the fence are involved in domestic disputes: with the Girl beckoning him from a third-floor window, Buster glides through the gate (revealed here for the first time), unseen past the squabbling parents, and effortlessly scales up the side of the house. For a brief moment of bliss Buster holds the Girl in his arms, but then seeing the Girl's father fast approaching up the stairs, he heads back out of the window. In an astonishing piece of acrobatics, Buster slides along the washing line, right over the yard and into the third-floor window of his parent's house, where he spins down and around on a banister which spews him back out onto the revolving clothes line, back across the yard and through the second-floor window of the neighbor's house: right into the lap of the Girl's father. A neat example of what Walter Kerr terms "The Keaton Curve,"[6] this spectacular moment also opens up the space above the backyards to a swift flow of horizontal motion, canceling the sense of vertical division imposed by the fence.

Buster's body literally transcends such division. The geometrical motif of vertical bisection introduced in the opening shot of the fence acquires a visual rhyme later in the film when the right half of Buster's face is colored black with paint. The situation is arrived at via a complex series of misapprehensions. Buster mistakes a cop for his neighbor and hits him over the head with a broom; the cop sees Buster, whose face happens to have been blackened with mud, and chases after him. Buster evades the cop by wiping off the mud on his mother's clean laundry and passing as a white man; the cop spies a passing black man walking down the street, bizarrely mistakes him for the culprit, and promptly arrests him (a nicely pointed gag on the myopic racism of the L.A.P.D.). Buster's mother sees her laundry has been dirtied and blames a painter up a ladder nearby who returns the compliment by pouring a bucket of black paint over her son; the black man has meanwhile escaped from the cop and the cop finds Buster, blackfaced once again (thus completing another Keaton Curve). As the cop drags him along, Buster uses his free hand to scrub the paint from just the left side of his face with a handkerchief, and the resulting appearance of racial duality so startles the cop that it allows Buster to escape. A rare use of close-up allows us to observe the precisely bisected face: half-black, half-white; a cutaway to the highly amused black man watching from over a fence underlines its connection to the bisected backyard. The compositional parallel between Buster's bi-colored face and the later shot of him perched on the fence foregrounds a certain indeterminacy in his relation to the social world, a world pictured as besieged by territorial division and racial category. Flung between extremes of white and black, permitted a place of rest on neither one side of the fence nor the other, Buster seeks the middle ground.

A distinction here might be made with Chaplin, who also can be said to bestride social categories: most centrally, the categories of tramp and aristocrat. A crucial difference, however, is the fluency with which Charlie inhabits both roles; his social proficiency creates the sense that he might pick and choose his identity as he pleases, as if it were a plaything of the self. By contrast, social identities seem more or less externally imposed onto Buster, as in *The Paleface*, in which Buster finds himself variously cast as both representative of white men *and* as an Indian tribesman. Not unlike the use of the fence in *Neighbors*, Buster's position of in-betweenness is articulated early on by his passage through the gate that divides the world of the white man from the Indian encampment. The Indians have been served an eviction notice from crooked white industrialists, and in response the Chief has decreed that the first white man to step through the gate shall be killed. This role is of course assigned to Buster, who, moments later, shuffles through the gate holding a butterfly net, and ironically

Half-black, half-white: Buster's bisected face in *Neighbors* (1921).

56

Buster passes through the gate, hunting butterflies in *The Paleface* (1922).

seals his own fate by fastening the wooden latch behind him. Later in the film, having been chased, captured and tied to the stake by the Indian tribe, Buster manages to survive a ritualistic burning (on account of his infinite resourcefulness: anticipating his destiny, he took time out from being chased to make himself some fire-resistant asbestos undergarments). This miraculous survival is granted respect and awe from the Indians, who accept him as one of the tribe, and in the next scene Buster emerges from a tepee and dons an eagle feather in his porkpie hat. Later still, Buster and the tribe are pursuing the white industrialists in an effort to defend the encampment. Buster gets separated from the others in a valley and is held at gunpoint by a white industrialist in top hat and tails who forces an exchange of clothes to allow his own escape. Now dressed in the businessman's suit, Buster is misrecognised by the tribe who spy him from the mountain top and fire arrows at him. In each of these moments, a new identity is foisted

57

onto Buster as a matter of how he appears, what he is wearing, where he happens to be. Social identity is shown to be radically circumstantial, as nothing more than the placement and appearance of the body at a given point in time.

Prior to Buster's entrance into the encampment, the film's opening sequence juxtaposes two civilizations, sketching difference by means of geometry. The Indian encampment is characterized by the triangular shape of tepees, finding visual echo in the roughly triangular outline of the Chief who sits smoking his pipe, in the crisscrossed diagonal sticks of the campfire, and in the prominent way the Chief summons his tribe by raising his arms up diagonally each side to form an X shape. The white industrialists, by contrast, are characterized by perpendicular lines: by the grid-like arrangement of their oak-paneled office interior, finding visual echo in the long black vertical lines of hanging curtains, and in the way the President of the Board stands bolt upright to direct his associates behind a horizontal desk. An ensuing flashback sequence shows the means by which the firm acquired the lease for the Indians' land: a thug waits for an Indian to emerge from the government land office before clouting him over the head with a truncheon. The connection between the ruthlessness of the oil sharks and the motif of perpendicular lines is here consolidated in the setting of this scene of violence directly against the long vertical slats of a fence. Such an association prepares us for Buster's entrance through the gate, similarly composed of vertical planks, and for the way in which Buster's circumstantial placement is taken as proof of allegiance to a brutal civilization. Equally important, however, is his passage *through* the gate and the careful locking of the latch behind him: a demonstration of naivety as to the significance of boundaries but also of quiet respectfulness for their upkeep. Just as for the butterfly he pursues, human frontiers do not seem to mean very much for Buster since he belongs solely to neither side.[7] Prominently cast against the dark wood of the fence, the amorphous white shape of Buster's butterfly net serves as contrast to the straight-lined geometry that characterizes *both* sides of the divide.

Indeed, following Buster's entrance, we seem more placed to notice *parallels* between the two societies through the use of geometry. When

Buster comes across the wooden stake, standing vertically in the dust outside the encampment, the line it casts and the violence it portends might remind us of the earlier scene of violence outside the government land office. Conversely, when Buster leads his now-loyal tribe to the white industrialists' office to demand justice, the triangular pylon-like structures dotted around the surrounding oilfield might remind us of the encampment tepees. In this way, the film sets Buster in discord not just to one society or another, but to society per se.

The demarcations and practices of society seem mystifying to Buster. When the Indian tribe first circle around Buster in a sacrificial dance, he fails to comprehend the meaning of this behavior. Observing with stoneface the tribesmen filing past, stomping and stooping to offer their sacrifice to the gods, Buster nods and claps to the rhythm of this dance of death, finally joining the back of the line and flourishing his hat like a showman in a vaudeville chorus. His response to baffling social practice is to observe and copy as best he can — but, unlike Chaplin's tramp, Buster is a poor mimic because he remains too far outside that practice, uncomprehendingly. The gesture of trying and humorously failing to become inconspicuous is characteristic of Buster's resigned attitude to a world that seems intent on chasing and conditioning him. His struggle for anonymity is similarly depicted later in the film as the attempt to remove himself from the center of things. Still attempting to escape the tribe who wish to ritualistically burn him, Buster disguises himself by wrapping himself up in a big patterned cloak, like a poncho, and tries to sneak out of the village. We see his efforts in uninterrupted far-shot, a perspective that maximizes the humor of his vain endeavors. At first the frame is empty except for Buster, and his chances of escape look promising. Just as he makes a dash for the farground, his efforts are halted by a group of Indians returning with wood for the pyre; he swiftly joins their group and helps with the stacking of timber in the center of the frame. Heading off screen-left, his escape is again cut short before he reaches the edge of the frame by more wood-collectors whose number he joins; the same happens when he tries to head off screen-right. Each time he makes a bid for freedom, Buster is returned to the center of the frame, to the ominous pyre which grows larger with every visit. What is pictured here is society as a smothering centripetal force, in which conformity is rewarded with anonymity and difference punished by fire.

The use of far-shot is wittily employed here as a means of maintaining the credibility of Buster's camouflage. It can be used in such a way because at distance the body is to some extent divested of the personality it embodies. When the tribe spy the figure in the valley wearing top hat and tails, we view that figure in an iris shot corresponding to the point-of-view of the head lookout. We know it to be Buster — but it must be conceded that, from that distance, it could be almost anybody. (Only the jaunty walk might give it away, but even that is more simply the bearing of someone satisfied with their material situation than it is distinctively Buster's way of walking.) The very same feature permits the abstraction of Keaton's geometrical far-shots. One

An amazing stunt and a starkly geometical image from *The Paleface* (1922). The speck visible halfway down the slope is Keaton's tumbling body.

of the most striking shots in all of Keaton's work can be found during Buster's flight from the Indians around halfway through *The Paleface*: a dramatic mountainside slope of white gravel that cuts diagonally through the frame, down the length of which — in extreme long shot — a tiny speck of a body bounds, twists and tumbles. The immediate power of this image is derived from the combination of the astonishing physical feat it documents and the starkness of its composition as accentuated by the line drawn by the tumbling figure. Similarly stark compositions can be found in the presentation of Buster's death-defying vertical fall down a precipice and his final desperate clamber across a rope bridge horizontally stretched across an abyss. In each case, the movement of Buster's body liberates geometrical form from its previously established societal associations to draw upon its formal power as such.

Much of the pleasure of Keaton's comedy arises from its capacity to reveal the world as not merely a social milieu or situational locale, but as a physical arena, wherein the body's immediate relation to surrounding topographical features constitutes the primary relation between self and world. It allows us to revisit the fun of certain childhood games based around hiding and dodging and running away in which a range of spatial and athletic possibilities of the body — size and shape, dexterity and litheness — are inventively played out in relation to features of the surrounding environment.[8] Towards the end of *The Goat*, Buster is cornered in a locked room with a gargantuan man bearing down on him. Things do not look good for Buster: not only is this the cop whose livid grasp he escaped earlier by offloading a ton of coal onto his back, but he also happens to be the forbidding father of Buster's girlfriend. The hopelessness of the situation is compounded when the father crushes the key to the locked door between thumb and forefinger, and advances towards Buster menacingly. The film cuts to a side-on perspective of the room with Buster backed against the frame's right-hand edge and the locked door at its extreme left, with only a dining table left between the father and Buster's gruesome fate. Uncoiling into action, Buster leaps onto the table in a flash, stepping up onto the father's shoulder

Up, up and away: with Joe Roberts as a springboard, Buster finds an escape from hopelessness in *The Goat* (1921).

and using that as a springboard to thrust his body through the tiny window *above* the locked door. This extraordinary maneuver is as remarkable for its acrobatic precision as it is for its foresight. Like Wittgenstein's famous duck-rabbit picture, a new aspect reveals itself besides the closing threat of violence and the sense of being hemmed-in: the diagonally-rising line of trajectory formed by the table, the man's shoulders and the window above the door.

It is Buster's capacity to see the situation in spatial terms, and his ability to act in accordance with that vision, that enables his sudden escape from an unpromising situation. The movement of Keaton's body up and across the frame refines our perception of the space, allowing us to see possibility where there had seemed none. In this respect it reverses the structure of an earlier sight gag which promises freedom in vain. Chased by a cop who believes him to be an escaped convict,

This tire is going nowhere. Keaton's playful eye at work in *The Goat* (1921).

Buster seeks a quick getaway by clinging to the spare tire on the back of a parked car which is about to be driven away. No sooner has Buster climbed aboard, however, than the car speeds off into the distance, leaving Buster and tire motionless: the tire is a standing sign advertising a nearby garage. Here Buster's perception matches our own, fooled by the camera's two-dimensional rendition of depth.[9] (A side-on view might have revealed to us the separateness of car and sign, but the camera's static frontal view instead invokes the limitations of embodied viewpoint in a world which can so easily deceive; Buster's perceptual alignment with the camera's view in this moment thus paradoxically captures at once his dreamlike detachment from the world *and* his inability to stand back from his involvement within it.)

Indeed, the film consistently foregrounds the deceptiveness of appearances and the duplicity of the photographic image, at once loyal and misleading. Buster's mistaken identity as a dangerous criminal at this point is the result of a photograph of his distinctive face having been circulated on wanted posters under the name Dead Shot Dan. This is once again the consequence of Buster's being in the wrong place at the wrong time. Happening to pass by the city jail just as the real Dead Shot Dan is having his picture taken for the Rogues' Gallery, Buster peers in through the bars; with the photographer distracted, all it now takes is for Dan to orchestrate the taking of Buster's picture instead of his own.[10] The momentary framing of Buster in the window anticipates the photograph's framing, pointing up the way photographs can so radically decontextualize by cropping and freezing the human figure. The distinction between still and moving pictures — introduced by the film camera's refusal to share the perspective of the still photographer's camera, and reiterated by the sequence in which the fake moustache Buster has pinned on to disguise his billboard image ungraciously wilts under the scrutiny of a cop — feeds into the film's broader interest in stillness and movement. In the opening sequence, Buster goes to take his place in a queue for bread behind a pair of very lifelike mannequins standing motionless on the sidewalk. The joke is cleverly organized so that our eye tends to be led by Buster's movement across the frame to join the back of the queue, and it consequently takes a second or two (about the time it takes for Buster to get in line) for our eye to settle before we register that these dummies are dummies. In other words, it is a play between movement and stillness that creates the pleasurable delay of recognition that is so central to the gag, itself poised around movement and its absence. Buster shuffles impatiently in line, shifts his weight, leans against the shop window, finally sits on the ledge and crosses his legs. Suddenly he thinks he spies some hint of forward motion, and jumps back into standing position ... but no, it was just his imagination. The moment captures a humorous and characteristic mix of obliviousness, vigilance and trust in Buster's relation to the world.

The gag finds an inverse rhyme soon after when Buster hides from a cop behind a cigarstore Indian figure. Celebrating his evasion, Buster strikes a match on the Indian, who abruptly turns to him and scolds

MAN O'WAR

The impossibility of staying still: the statue starts to bend beneath Buster's weight in *The Goat* (1921).

him for doing so. This time we fully share Buster's failure to distinguish between the animate and the inanimate world — partly on account of its impeccable execution, partly on account of its utter inexplicability. Nevertheless, the very inconspicuousness of the Indian introduces the possibility that stillness rather than movement might best serve the need for evasion. Diving beneath a parked car in a subsequent scene, Buster lies flat and still in its shadow: the perfect camouflage from the ever-present cops ... until, that is, the car starts up and begins to drive away, leaving Buster exposed in the bright sunlight. Instantly, he amends his strategy, clinging to the car's rear spare tyre and allowing it to drag him away from the clutches of the cops. The world moves on; Buster must move with it. A little later, Buster tries to hide at the public inauguration of a new statue; when the statue of a horse is unveiled, Buster is astride it, hand raised to his head as if scanning the horizon, hoping that nobody will notice him. To exacerbate his utter conspicuousness, the statue is made of wet clay, and the legs of the horse slowly bend and buckle beneath his weight. The image exemplifies Buster's restless relation to a world in continual flux, where the only thing to do is creatively react, moment by moment, to its changing state.

3

Body and Clothes: Harold Lloyd

They were like my nose, my mouth, my eyes.
They were something that was part of me. I never took my glasses
off....[1]

> (Harold Lloyd, referring to his character's
> famous horn-rimmed spectacles.)

Trouser-tearing, hat-tipping, tie-fiddling and cross-dressing are
recurring pleasures of physical comedy, and with these kinds of activity clothes constitute one of the genre's most significant resources. Each
of the major silent film clowns — Charlie Chaplin, Harold Lloyd, Buster
Keaton and Harry Langdon — employed a distinctive style of costume
that set him apart from the other film comedians. To differing extents,
these costumes also served to single these figures out from their surrounding milieu. When Chaplin rounds the street corner for the first
time early in *City Lights* (1931), he is instantly set apart from the bustling
crowd by his distinctive costume — derby hat, cane, shabby jacket and
sack-like trousers. He becomes the center of our attention partly
because of his visual difference — the same difference that places him
on the peripheries of society. He strolls at a pace that only a millionaire or a tramp could afford, and his outfit perfectly suits the blend of
those two roles that is intrinsic to his every gesture. When the evident
pride he takes in his gentleman-like attire — manifested in the mannered way he fiddles with his cuffs and tucks his cane under his arm —
renders him the figure of amusement for a couple of newsboys, Charlie

snaps his fingers in retaliation, removing a cloth finger from his tattered glove so as to execute the snap more proficiently. Chaplin's use of his clothes here perfectly captures the humorous sense of the character's dignity-in-destitution, the very raggedness of his attire providing the opportunity for a display of haughty superiority.

The clothes define the clown: mark him out from others, shape his body and delineate his identity. The impression of an infantile physiognomy in Harry Langdon results as much from his moon-like face, cowish eyes, unsteady posture and uncommitted gestures as from the effect of his poorly-fitting clothes, which fashion a middle-aged man's stout figure into the awkwardly-proportioned shape of a toddler. At the start of Frank Capra's *Long Pants* (1927), Harry, pudgy in his too-tight jacket and schoolboy shorts, sits in the attic and wistfully imagines himself bedecked in the suave military uniform of a chivalric prince, a regal cape flowing out behind him as he chases a playful damsel around a fairytale setting, scaling the castle wall for a dynamic kiss on the balcony. The idea that a mere change of clothes might transform this

Harold Lloyd wearing his famous spectacles.

dumpy dreamer into a man of action and romance is surreally developed moments later when Father decides that Harry has come of age sufficiently to be dressed in a pair of long pants (he'll grow into them, Father says). The recurrent occasion of Harry being dressed by others — by his father and then by a city vamp in *Long Pants*, by a couple of thugs in *The Strong Man* (1926), into his walking outfit in *Tramp, Tramp, Tramp* (1926) — epitomises the babyish passivity of his body, visible in the limpness

Dignity in destitution: the distinctive attire of Charlie Chaplin in *City Lights* (1931).

of his joints and the plasticity of his limbs. But despite this seeming mutability, and despite the array of costume changes in a given Langdon feature — into prison uniform, the leotard of a circus strong man, the tuxedo of a groom — his body remains impervious, fixed at the core in its mélange of infant and adult, refusing to be shoved fully into one role or the other. The long pants will always be too long and the short pants too short. Langdon's stubborn thickset torso will not yield to the transformative potential of clothes, and these clothes respond by continually hampering his development, as when a gun gets stuck in his trousers, or when his braces latch themselves around a tree branch, or when his overlong sleeves render his stumpy fingers incapable of removing coins from his pocket. The prison ball-and-chain attached to his ankle in *Tramp, Tramp, Tramp* is merely an extension of the way other articles of dress treat him. Doing the work of a baby's pacifier, clothes reify his body's inertia.

For Buster Keaton, the relationship between his body and its draperies is equally, if differently, hostile. Clothes seem intent on colonising Buster's body, sapping its uniqueness and pushing it into

Harry Langdon as a chain-gang prisoner in *Tramp, Tramp, Tramp* (1926).

line. In *Steamboat Bill Jr.* (1928), Buster has returned from several years at college in Boston to the no-nonsense small-town boating community in which his father is a well-known boatsman. Father and son set out to meet one another at the station: Father in his practical cloth cap, long weatherproof jacket and a grubby workman's shirt with a packet of cigs in the top pocket; Buster in a striped jacket, patterned waistcoat and baggy trousers, a high-collared shirt with a spotty bow tie, and an artist's beret perched on his head — no doubt the fashion in Boston, but singularly unbefitting to Buster's diffident body. He sports a pencil moustache and has a ukulele tucked under his arm; Father's disapproval is not hidden. Having first dragged his son to the barber's (to remove "that barnacle off his lip"), he now marches him to a hat shop where they might find an article of headwear more suitable for a boatsman's son. Positioned in front of the mirror, a stream of hats are passed from shop owner to Father, each hat enjoying a brief sojourn

A cheap bible salesman or a fairground hustler? Buster's trouble with hats in *Steamboat Bill Jr.* (1928).

on the top of Buster's head. Shot in a long static take, and from the alienating perspective of the mirror into which Buster gazes, subtly adjusting his facial features to the self-image thrust upon him, the mise-en-scène reflects Buster's incredulity at his own powerlessness to measure up. Every new hat makes Buster look more ridiculous than the last. A large straw hat with a flat crown and striped ribbon around the base makes him look like a cheap bible salesman or maybe a fairground hustler. A bulbous grey bowler smacks of a yokel trying to make good in the city. An indented stetson riding high on the head bestows the air of a pious deputy, the kind that gets accidentally shot in small-town saloons. None of the hats seem to fit — Father makes to widen one hat by wrenching the sides apart, and the stubborn brim of one straw hat just won't remain comfortably up or down. But we understand this to be not a problem of an awkwardly-shaped head; rather, it is indicative of a physicality that refuses to fully assent to any particular identity. This is not wilful rebellion on Buster's part; he just doesn't quite fit into what clothes confer.

Buster seems to understand the social necessity of clothes, but, as a man more at ease in wide open spaces, he can't get along with something so clingy so close to the skin. Clothes fail to accommodate the body's own wish for comfort and dignity. Keaton seems *almost* apposite to period costume — there's something about his eyes that resembles the gaze of sitters in old photographs, helpless to their fate — but even then, clothes are a nuisance he has to contend with. In the 1830s setting of *Our Hospitality* (1923), Buster is aboard the Outbound Limited in a cramped train carriage, squashed in beside a demure southern belle to whom he has coyly taken a shine. With cravat and frock shirt, he is dressed as the upright gentleman, a proper escort for this respectable young lady. He holds in his hand a large funnel-shaped top hat, which would complete the look, but — due to the low carriage-ceiling and the largeness of the hat — he can't lift it up to place on top of his head. Ingenious as ever, and always willing to adapt to his environmental limitations, Buster pushes the flat-top of the hat against the ceiling and squeezes his head down underneath it. Job done — except that no sooner has he achieved this than the carriage jolts over a bump and the hat is plunged down over his eyes. With the physical size of the hat as an index of social status and masculinity, Buster fails to match up to its requirements. The southern belle looks at him, unimpressed. Humiliated, Buster tugs the hat off his head, slams it down in resentment and sticks on his less-respectable-but-more-accommodating-to-cramped-spaces porkpie hat. Made famous in his early two-reelers such as *Cops* and *One Week* (both 1921), this porkpie hat seems to follow Keaton around, haunting him with his own past image. It even finds its way onto Keaton's head in the *Steamboat Bill Jr* hat-shop sequence: Buster recognises it in the mirror, eyes aghast, shivers, and claws it off, lest a legion of city cops should return to haul him away.

Whereas for Keaton, clothes remain as external to the self as any other physical object, Chaplin's entrance in *The Gold Rush* (1925) — a solitary figure in black against a backdrop of white snow — portrays a comparably stark dichotomy of self and world, but one in which clothes belong firmly to the realm of the former. The dramatic documentary-style opening sequence — depicting the harsh landscape of Alaska forbidding a multitude of gold-prospectors to pass — gives way to the familiar appearance of the little Tramp, decked out in his usual get-up, moseying around a snow-covered mountain ledge. The comic incongruity between urban garments and wild environment is balanced by the Tramp's apparent ignorance of their incompatibility: his clothes seem so natural to him that he simply fails to notice their unsuitability for the terrain. One can imagine Keaton's treatment of a similar scenario involving a visual gag on the absurd appearance of Old Stoneface in Eskimo gear; Chaplin's clothes declare an ethic of adapting the world to his requirements, rather than the other way round. Having cheerfully negotiated a deadly ravine (by sliding down on his bottom), Charlie stops to lean on his trusty cane, only for it to disappear, to his surprise, into the snow. What a silly place to put a snowdrift.

The Tramp's instinctual reliance upon his cane here is symptomatic of the way in which his clothes are perceived as part of his body. Indeed, James Naremore, discussing Chaplin's expressive use of his cane, comments that it functions as a "virtual part of ... [his] anatomy."[2] This impression heightens the cannibalistic connotations of the episode later

Boot-iful! Chaplin's famous Thanksgiving supper in *The Gold Rush* (1925).

in which the Tramp's boot is served up as Thanksgiving supper. The inter-association between clothes, food and the body — one of the film's most odd and sustained thematic explorations, taking the form of something like a riddle — finds its locus with this episode. The pleasure Charlie takes in devouring his boot is funny not just because he spectacularly transforms a piece of old leather and a set of rusty nails into a bountiful and apparently delicious meal (a testament to the powers of the imagination to supersede the demands of the body), but also because he is partaking of himself, incorporating himself like the worm who eats his own tail. One bodily need — the need to eat — has taken precedence over another — the need to stay warm and dry — and the former has been bizarrely satisfied by the customary answer to the latter (hunger has been satisfied by clothes). This finds a complement when Charlie solves the problem of being cold by placing his now-bootless foot in the oven — the customary place for the solution to hunger.

This is the third instance in which Charlie's body has been rendered as food. Earlier on in the film, a famished Charlie tips salt on his fingers as if seasoning himself, and earlier still, his cabin mate, Big Jim, attempts to seize a chicken leg from Charlie's grasp and sinks his teeth into the little Tramp's thumb. Each occasion anticipates Big Jim's hunger-fuelled hallucination of Charlie as an enormous chicken — an example of the imagination existing at the service of the body, and the most overt case of the body being taken for food. Big Jim's desperate scrambling to eat his companion is interrupted by a grizzly bear who bursts into the cabin just as Charlie is wrestling Big Jim, decked out in his fur-coat, to the ground. Somehow the bear takes Big Jim's place, and mistaking the animal's natural pelt for Big Jim's fur-coat — the body being mistaken for clothes, this time — Charlie continues wrestling this beast to the ground, looking now even more likely to end up as someone's dinner. Upon realising his error, however, Charlie adroitly picks up the cabin rifle and, in a swift reversal of the roles of predator and prey, secures a feast for both men. Such patterning humorously invokes an enigmatic relationship between clothes, food and the body as a way of dramatising competing bodily needs. At a most basic level, food and clothes fulfil the respective human requirements of sustenance, and protection against a hostile environment. But Chaplin's gestures of taken-for-granted connoisseurship when tucking into his boiled boot exemplify the way in which the basic satisfaction of a need can be figured as the achievement of opulence.[3] Similarly, as the opening sequence demonstrates, the little Tramp can endure — barely even seeming to notice! — the hardships of the Alaskan climate wearing little more than a threadbare canvas suit; not because he is superhuman, but because his identity is assured by these clothes, and this utter self-assurance allows such imaginative scope that a severe mountain trek can become a stroll in the park.

The finale of *The Gold Rush* conveys the extent to which the identity of the Tramp is bound to his clothes. By the end of the film, the Tramp has become a millionaire, now swaggering across the deck of an ocean liner in a tailored suit, a glossy top hat and not one but *two* expensive-looking coats. His old walk has gone. His expressive facial

Chaplin as millionaire near the end of *The Gold Rush* (1925).

twitches have been traded for a tightened look of glazed affluence, his light quick shrugs displaced by hunched shoulders heavy with fur. When old habit briefly resurfaces and Charlie bends down to pick up a still-smoking cigar butt from the deck, his fellow millionaire Big Jim whacks it out of his hand, offering him his pick of a rack of six full Cubans. Occasionally, out of common view, he scratches himself; as if his body were itching to get out of this silk and back into his flea-bitten rags. The opportunity presents itself: wanting to capture the rags-to-riches angle, the press want a photograph of Charlie as the Tramp. The change of clothes initiates an immediate return to his former and essential self. As he proudly brushes down his shabby suit, or himself inside it, he spots Big Jim flirting with a manicurist. He looks on for a moment, with the lingering stare of an outsider, at this scene which minutes before he had been part of, before breaking into his familiar cheeky grin with a mischievous raising of the eyebrows and a teasing "now-now" finger of mock-disapproval. He impishly spins around on

Return of the Tramp: Chaplin interrupts Mack Swain's manicure (administered by Barbara Pierce) in *The Gold Rush* (1925).

his toes, dispenses a playful up-and-out back-kick to Big Jim's face, and waddles off. The Tramp has triumphantly returned.

Chaplin's identity is as tied to his clothes as it is to his body. His distinctive bandy-legged walk — that most characteristic application of his body, defining of Chaplin — would not be what it is without the baggy trousers ballooning at the thighs and the oversized shoes bulging at the outward-pointing toes. In discussing the genesis of the Tramp character in his autobiography, Charles Chaplin writes:

> I thought I would dress in baggy pants, big shoes, a cane and a derby hat.... The moment I was dressed, the clothes and the make-up made me feel the person he was. I began to know him, and by the time I walked on to the stage he was fully born. [...] With the clothes on I felt he was a reality, a living person.[4]

Chaplin's clothes are so constitutive of his identity that they seem of a piece with his body, in perfect accord with his postures and gestures. Charles Baudelaire, in his famous text "The Painter of Modern Life," makes the following observation about the sight of a beautiful woman:

> All the things that adorn woman, all the things that go to enhance her beauty, are part of herself.... She is a harmonious whole, not only in her carriage and in the movement of her limbs, but also in the muslins and gauzes, in the vast and iridescent clouds of draperies in which she envelops herself....[5]

The sense of unity between body and apparel praised by Baudelaire here seems to fit the way in which Chaplin's clothes appear as part of himself. In the case of Chaplin, however, this unity is less the upshot of his beauty than of his deftness or affiliation with physical objects. Just as, in *The Gold Rush*, a couple of bread rolls on forks can become imbued with such life and personality that they seem an extension of his body, Chaplin's clothes are at once vivified and stripped of their autonomy by the way he uses and wears them: they become part of him.[6]

Yet physical comedy is seemingly obsessed with the *divisibility* of body and clothes, not least in Chaplin's films. Even while Chaplin's clothes are emblematic, even constitutive of him, they are undoubtedly physical things, and hence divisi-

Baggy pants, derby hat and that bendy cane...: Chaplin unmistakable in *The Gold Rush* (1925).

ble from him: his tattered glove slides off his finger, his hat falls off his head, his boot gets put in the oven. We might recall more generally the wealth of gags in Hollywood slapstick in which trousers fall down, crazy disguises are donned and thrown off, jackets and dresses are torn away from the wearer. What is the source of this obsession? In the College Ball sequence from Harold Lloyd's *The Freshman* (1925), Harold, an over-eager college freshman and the unwitting campus stooge, arrives at the Fall Frolic wearing a defective tuxedo (the tailor has suffered from dizzy spells while working on it and as a result the seams are only basted; he accompanies Harold to the ball with a needle and thread, just in case). Of course, as the ball proceeds, the suit rips and tears and falls apart in the most unfortunate places and spaces. Despite the efforts of the tailor to resurrect it, the tuxedo progressively falls apart from Harold's body until, encircled by his peers, events finally conspire to rid him of his tailcoat and trousers. The tuxedo confers physical form to Harold's dream of becoming accepted and popular. Harold's arrival at college immediately marks his separateness from the campus in-crowd, and establishes his double wish to become assimilated into that crowd, and at the same time to stand out from it, as a distinctive and exemplary member of it. The tension inherent to the ideal of the singular everyman is captured in Harold's conflicting desires to fit in and stand out: a potent rendering of the paradoxes of the American Dream, where success is a measure of both conformity and uniqueness. The gradual, humorous, painful disintegration of the tuxedo is the crushing of that dream; the divisibility of clothes and body gives voice to its hollowness.

Upon his arrival at the ball, Harold is handed a heavily-tassled fez to wear on his head to mark his status as the host of the party (a role which in Harold's mind confirms the esteem others hold him in — in fact, it conveys the opposite; the hat might as well spell out "dunce"). Put on display, and greeted with mock cheers, Harold stands in his timebomb tuxedo at the threshold of the party and excitedly waves. As his arm goes up, the material tears around his armpit; he quickly lowers it, mortified. The gesture and its adverse effect are telling. The very over-eagerness of Harold's gesticulations, designed to ingratiate himself with the group he aspires towards, in fact accelerates the demise

That's torn it: Harold Lloyd rips his jacket in *The Freshman* (1925).

of the suit and hence of his chances of becoming one of their number. A moment later, he tries waving again, this time grabbing his pocket handkerchief to shake; the pocket rips off with the handkerchief and falls to the floor. Harold surreptitiously shoves the pocket under a rug with his feet — the insertion of a close-up shot of this action capturing the desperation of his attempt to keep some vestige of privacy — and tries to shove the handkerchief into his jacket pocket, only to realise that this pocket is not sewn at the bottom. He tries to look casual, leaning against a pillar with a smile (thinly masking his discomfort) and his thumb tucked inside his jacket; the waistcoat snaps at the shoulder and droops down, mocking the posture's claims towards masculine poise. Then, in swiftly trying to cover his shame by tugging his jacket around his chest, a gash materializes down the seam of his back. Each attempt to conceal reveals further; Harold's determination to keep himself in one piece in fact hastens the inevitable schism.

3. Body and Clothes: Harold Lloyd

The disintegration of Harold's tuxedo, as an avowal of its separateness from his body, physicalizes and explores through comic means
the familiar experience of feeling detached from a social façade we feel
obliged to keep up. To this end, the suit's rejection of Harold's body
strikes us as both cruel and apt. The tuxedo, and all that it stands for,
is a sham. The physical divisibility of body and clothes lends credence
to the idea of clothes as a deceptive front, concealing the naked body
beneath as a figure of the true self, that which cannot be presented
without embellishment. In this case, how do we understand the final
shot of *The Freshman*, which provides us with the amusing and ambiguous image of a fully-clothed Harold taking a shower? Harold has finally
won the admiration of his peers by somehow scoring the winning
touchdown in an important college football game. He has also won the
love of the girl — although we understand the girl to have been won
over by more than his success at football. In the locker room after the
match, Harold, still dressed in football gear, rejects the smothering
embraces of the crowd in order to find a place of privacy to read a love
note that has been passed to him from his girl. He finds the shower
room, and, reading the note in amorous rapture, leans backwards onto
the shower lever to release the flow of water. Busy dreaming, Harold
seems unaware that he has not removed his clothes, or else that water
falls over him from above. As the final gag in the film, and an odd one
at that, the weight given to Harold's obliviousness to the incongruity
of wearing clothes in the shower invites us to reconsider it as more than
just a demonstration of how Harold's dreaminess will continue to distance him from the surrounding world. The gag serves as a sort of coda
to the primary narrative of the film, which is Harold's achievement of
popularity. As such, it might be seen partially to qualify Harold's success by implying his continuing delusion: does he perceive his football-
hero identity as so native to him now that he can mistake these clothes
for his own skin? Will Harold ever be able to unclothe himself— to
remove the material paraphernalia of his social ambition? The college
ball sequence and the shower gag are in some sense opposites of one
another. The first takes place in the public sphere under the scrutiniz-
ing gaze of his peers; the second takes place in as private a space as he

It's only a shower: Harold Lloyd fully clothed in *The Freshman* (1925).

can find, where he can supposedly be himself, at last. The college ball is traumatic; the shower is blissful. In the first, Harold struggles to keep his clothes on to convey an impression of unity; in the second, Harold's sense of that unity is such that he no longer feels *dressed*.

In failing to distinguish between his clothes and his body, Harold is in some sense continuing the self-delusion that has characterised his behaviour throughout the film. During the preceding fateful football game, the unathletic Harold sits on the sideline bench, duped into believing himself to be a substitute player rather than the waterboy he really is — clothes can lie, even to the wearer. His self-blindness is typified when an on-field player beckons Harold in response to another player's football pullover being ripped to shreds: Harold interprets the gesture as a call-up, when in fact the waterboy is being beckoned not for his body but for his clothes. The comic confusion of the episode is amplified by Harold's jubilant removal of his outer sweater before racing onto the pitch in his sports pullover, only to find that he must remove *that* pullover and hand it to the teammate with the torn kit. Where the first sweater-removal expresses his jubilation at acceptance, the second removal seems to seal his complete rejection. Against all odds, Harold is nonetheless called up to play, as a desperate last resort on the part of the coach. His white under-sweater distinguishes him from both teams who wear coloured shirts, underscoring Harold's doggedness as an individualistic drive to prove himself: he snatches the ball from the hands of a teammate at one point, and lines up with the opposing team in a moment of dizzy determination. The motivated costuming of Harold in white inflects with significance the decision to stage a struggle for individual recognition within a team sport, providing another example of the tension between fitting into a group and standing out from it.

This tension, discussed earlier with reference to Harold's desire to become the singular everyman, is central to Lloyd's persona.

When the landlady (unknown actress) comes calling, Harold and friend are disguised as overcoats in *Safety Last* (1923).

Accounts of his development as a film comedian stress the importance of his decision to abandon his Lonesome Luke costume — which was derivative of Chaplin in seeking to reverse each aspect of the Tramp's costume — in favour of his "glasses" outfit, a more naturalistic attire conforming to and redefining the American Everyman.[7] The horn-rimmed glasses are his costume's sole distinguishing feature, and yet it is a feature that signifies his ordinariness rather than eccentricity. Lloyd is immediately distinguished from the other silent comedians by his relatively undistinguished man-on-the-street attire. He is not dressed as a clown. There is nothing grotesque about his appearance. He can appear among the day-trippers at Coney Island in *Speedy* (1927) without looking at all out of place; if unreasonable things would just stop happening to him, he could melt into the crowd. Harold's desire to fit in to his surroundings is given neat visual form in a moment from *Safety Last* (1923). Harold and his flatmate can't afford to pay the rent; the stern landlady, come to demand her payment, knocks at the door. Harold and friend leap up, grab their overcoats off their hooks, put them on and promptly hang the coats — with themselves inside — back onto the wall. The landlady bursts in to the room but fails to see anything but a bare apartment and a couple of overcoats hanging beside the door.

The notion of clothes as camouflage recurs in *Safety Last*. The sequence in which, late for work at the department store, Harold dresses in drag to disguise himself as a mannequin so as to pass unnoticed by his belligerent boss (an extension of the idea of clothes sapping any semblance of life from the wearer) finds a weird complement later in the film when a drunk passing a department store window mistakes a stylishly-dressed mannequin for the Lady from "The Follies" (raising the inverse and uncanny idea that clothes can bestow a semblance of life). Harold too is victim to the deceptive powers of clothes. Recognising his old friend from back home in the uniform of a cop, Harold congratulates his friend Jim on the rise in social status signalled by his clothes. Moments later, Harold wishes to play a prank on his other friend, Bill. Seeking to prove to Bill that he has some power over the cops so that he can "get away with anything," he points over at the cop and convinces Bill to shove him over backwards. What Harold has failed to notice is that the cop over there is no longer his friend Jim but another cop — dressed, as cops tend to be, in exactly the same attire. In their noisy assertions of identity (a cop; a mannequin; a lady from "The Follies"), clothes can mislead by directing attention away from the face and body as more faithful manifestations of identity. The interchangeability of clothes, made possible by their lack of uniqueness, redoubles their capacity to deceive.

Harold is counting on such a capacity in the *Freshman* ball. That sequence is an extended account of the way in which clothes are made to cloak the self as much as express it, and of the way in which the desire to achieve the appearance of a united public front might entail the surrender of oneself to one's clothes. Clothes represent the public aspect of the body, flesh its private aspect, hidden from view. When the reconciliation of public and private is unmanageable, either the clothes must give way, or the body must perform grotesque contortions, or both. The demarcation between public and private in the sequence is partly defined architecturally: Harold stands awkwardly on the threshold between the party and the lobby area (where he can be himself, and where the cloakroom girl values people for who they are, hence she unburdens them of their clothes), and later on, the tailor is secretly positioned behind a curtain, where he can act as Harold's superego. At one point at the party, while flirting with a girl, Harold has unconsciously fiddled with the loose thread in his trousers (the innuendo could hardly be more pronounced!) and his trousers have come apart down the seam. We rejoin him sitting at a table with the girl, the bottom half of his body obscured from view and the curtain directly behind him. The cut "behind the scenes" to the other side of the curtain reveals the tailor busily sewing the trouser-seam back together: Harold's legs appear horizontally through the threshold, bent double underneath his torso, unbeknownst to the public world. That such covert contortion is necessary to sustain both public and private halves of the self speaks volumes about Harold's desire to appear whole, or be whole. It is as if the tailor is sewing *him* back together, which justifies why, at one point, the needle is accidentally driven into Harold's flesh. Clothes redefine

Harold continues to socialize while the tailor (Joseph Harrington) sews his pants in *The Freshman* (1925).

the perimeters of the body; it can be difficult to know where clothes end and the body begins.

Both *The Freshman* and *Safety Last* arrange into coherent narratives a string of gags based around clothes and their relationship to identity and the body. In *Safety Last*, clothes enter into two of the film's major thematic patterns. The first is that of misidentification, a pattern which is established in the opening sequence with the viewer's mistaking of a railway station for a jail and a leave-taking for an execution, and then with Harold's misidentification of a baby for a suitcase and a cart for a train. The film's celebrated conclusion, in which Harold inadvertently climbs a skyscraper, brings this pattern to a close in an arrangement of fate that prevents the makeshift plan — for Harold's friend Bill to secretly replace him as the human spider at the Level 2 windows, swapping jacket and hat so the watching crowd will believe it to be the same man — from going into operation. In other

3. Body and Clothes: Harold Lloyd

Harold Lloyd hangs from the clock in *Safety Last* (1923).

words, the plan for misidentification fails; Harold distinguishes himself by (somehow!) climbing to the top. (Incidentally, the famous moment when Harold desperately clings to the clock is the moment he loses his hat; this apparently insignificant detail, by portending Harold's own fall with the downwards trajectory of his hat, subtly relates the divisibility of clothes to the precariousness of the body itself.)

The second thematic pattern in which clothes play a role concerns the objectification of people — a common interest in physical comedy, but intriguingly explored here with regard to the way Harold repeatedly transforms *himself* into an object, such as when he lies down in the road, posing as an unconscious traffic accident victim in order for an ambulance to take him to work on time. The sequence in which he disguises himself as a mannequin and the gag with the overcoats are two other examples of this phenomenon; it is as if by submitting to the shapes and meanings dictated by clothes, one is forced to share their inertness. (The dead-eyed facial expressions of catwalk fashion models might be seen to support this intuition!) During a sequence at Harold's workplace, a department store where he sells fabric, a mob of unruly old women, each desperate to buy some material, squabble over pieces of cloth and for Harold's attention. At one point two women grab Harold by the jacket and tug him to and fro as if he were a rag doll; he quietly ducks out of the jacket and leaves them to fight over it. The pleasure of this moment lies in the swift and effortless division of clothes from body, in the way Harold rebuffs their objectification of him by declaring his separateness from cloth.

The use of clothes in *The Freshman* revolves largely around the theme of integrity: personal, social and bodily. In an early sequence, Harold daydreams over a book entitled "Clever College Clothes" and over a copy of the 1924 college yearbook where a photograph of The Most Popular Man in College, Chet Trask, holds pride of place. In a shot of the photograph corresponding to Harold's optical point-of-view and his desiring imagination, the face of Chet melts into the face

Store-crazy ladies fight over Harold in *Safety Last* (1923).

of Harold, while the body of the figure (below the neck) remains constant. The partiality of this overlay already implies that Harold's desire for social integrity (in this case, popularity) will entail a compromise of his personal integrity (a shedding of his own identity). Furthermore, the fact that, in a photograph, the body and clothes of the wearer are visually indistinguishable means that it is ambiguous whether Harold's desire-to-be-other is surfacing in a desire merely for Chet's clothes, or also for his body. At any rate, the severance of Harold's head from his own body implies a sacrifice of bodily integrity that anticipates the contortions of the college ball. It is in this sequence that Harold's anxieties about presenting an integral self mutate into the desperation to keep himself together, which means striving to keep his body and clothes in one piece. The final shot, of Harold fully-dressed in the shower, suggests the eventual achievement of this unity, but it does so with the additional implication that such an achievement is as ludicrous as taking a shower with clothes on.

Each of the comedians I have discussed here draws upon the divisibility of body and clothes for comic and significant purpose. Langdon and Keaton depict clothes as essentially antagonistic to the body — bullish in the case of Langdon, alien in the case of Keaton. Chaplin's clothes, by contrast, appear as part of his body — this is partly a feature of their expressiveness, partly of the way he uses clothes, seeming somehow to incorporate them. The divisibility of clothes, for Chaplin, serves as a counterpoint to this impression, a reminder of his deftness in making objects seem an extension of the self. Harold Lloyd's comedy negotiates both conceptions of the relation of clothes to the body, maintaining an awareness both of the way in which clothes vividly form part of the body we see, sculpting it and shifting its identity, and, at the same time, of the sense in which clothes constitute something separate to the body. Clothes are integral to the body and its projection of self and yet separable from that body. By the end of *The Freshman*, it is as if Harold has assimilated his clothes into his body, despite the empirical fact that these clothes are just as divisible from him as the college ball tuxedo. Clothes are depicted as an uncanny supplement to the body: an addition that becomes part of the whole. In this way, clothes are regarded as *prosthetic* to the body. It seems to me more than coincidental that after Harold Lloyd lost his forefinger and thumb to an explosion on the set of *Haunted Spooks* in 1919, he always hid his deformity, wearing gloves in society and a prosthetic hand in films, which he took great pains to conceal from the camera.[8] This condition must have made him intensely aware of the specific way in which something can be part of the body and yet not part of it. Indeed, the fact that the body is not a complete, sealed and indivisible entity is a fact we are faced with every time we trim our nails or cut our hair. In drawing upon the notion of clothes as an uncanny supplement, as prosthetic to the body as the body can seem to the self, Lloyd's comedy can extend its exploration of the theme of integrity to challenge the very idea of the body's wholeness.

4

Body and Machine: A Wrench in the Works

This chapter will consider how the relationship between the body and machinery is played out in sequences from three physical comedies featuring some of the most prominent performers in the genre. My analysis will address the detail of these moments, drawing parallels and differences between presentations and uses of the body in its engagement with particular machines, to develop a sense of the range of ways in which the relation between technology and the body is comically presented. Henri Bergson's ambitious but rather schematic treatise on comedy led him to claim that "the attitudes, gestures and movements of the human body are laughable in exact proportion as that body reminds us of a mere machine."[1] What is striking about the sequences under consideration here, each of which I claim to be in important ways characteristic of each respective performer, is that in setting the body directly against and in interaction with technology, the comic effect tends to draw at least as much upon the body's distinction from the machine, in terms of attitudes, gestures and movements, as on its resemblance to it.

In *Get Out and Get Under* (1920), Harold Lloyd is in love. The primary object of his passion and affection, however, is not flesh and blood, but a shiny Model T Ford, kept under cloth in his wooden garage and lovingly cared for with oilcan and wash mitt. Having entered

91

Man and machine: Charlie Chaplin in a publicity still for *Modern Times* (1936).

the garage and removed the cloth, Harold gazes adoringly at his beloved machine, checks the temperature of the room is not too cold for the dear thing and gently caresses the door frame — not forgetting to polish away the offending fingerprints (the body is barely fit to touch this machine, let alone dominate it). Clearly sharing Harold's fondness towards the machine, the film follows Harold's race across the countryside to take up his leading role in an amateur theatrical performance for which he is already late. As the journey gets underway, he is further impeded by unintentional detours, unrelenting motorcycle cops and, as the title suggests, car breakdowns. One potential complication arises when the car goes over a bump and Harold's suitcase, containing his costume for the performance, falls off the back into the road. Not wishing to lose time in stopping (or risk being unable to start the temperamental thing again), Harold bounds from the driver's seat with the car still engaged in gear and sprints back along the long straight road to retrieve the case. No sooner has he — remarkably! — caught up with the driverless car again and thrown the case onto the back, than the case bounces out once more and back onto the road. With the car still in full flow, Harold repeats the mad-dash retrieval, leaps back into the driver's seat and resumes his journey with no time lost. Crucial to the comic effect is the swiftness of the double rescue and the camera's position in relation to the action: the entire feat is shown in an uninterrupted frontal tracking shot that remains equidistant to the moving car as Harold runs off into the distance, collects the case, and hurtles back to the car, twice over, as if to flaunt the body's dominion over the machine by its ability to disengage from it and yet repeatedly reconquer it in a single fluid movement. Indeed, one result of staying parallel to the driverless Ford in a single take is to emphasize the car's steady automatism in relation to Harold's frantic scurrying and gathering, and so to stress a distinction between the rigidity of the machine and the flexibility of the unaided human body. On the other hand, Harold's characteristic go-getter determination and boundless energy appear here, more than ever, as a mechanistically single-minded drive to succeed, while the retrieval's repetition might be seen to resemble the back-and-forth motion of a piston.

The balance is finely struck because there is nothing particularly mechanical about Lloyd's performative style. One could imagine Keaton's enactment of the same stunt, recalling James Agee's evocative description of his body:

Harold Lloyd races to collect his fallen luggage (as the car drives on unattended) in *Get Out and Get Under* (1920).

> His short-legged body was all sudden, machinelike angles, governed by a daft aplomb. When he swept a semaphore arm to point, you could almost hear the electrical impulse in the signal block. When he ran from a cop his transitions from accelerating walk to easy jogtrot to brisk canter to headlong gallop to flogged-piston sprint ... were as distinct and as soberly in order as an automatic gearshift.[2]

Lloyd's body, by contrast, is more straightforwardly organic: when he runs to recover the suitcase, his gestures are irregular and erratic, the movement of his limbs frenetic rather than methodical. The gag thus points neither to a mechanical union between man and machine, nor to their complete sovereignty from one another, but to a symbiotic relationship. Each party needs the other: Harold needs the car to get to the theatre on time, while the car needs Harold to stay in one piece (the car veers dangerously towards the verge each time before Harold's re-requisition of the steering wheel). This symbiosis mutates into a more parasitic relationship as the film proceeds and as the Ford

Car Eats Man! Fixing the motor in *Get Out and Get Under* (1920).

becomes less obliging. The extent of the car's dependency on Harold (likened at one stage to a drug habit when he injects the engine with a junkie's heroin syringe to give it a kick-start) is illustrated when it decides to break down and we see Harold reaching further and further inside the bonnet with his wrench, finally disappearing entirely from view. The impression of the car having swallowed Harold whole figures the machine as an external parasite, stepping up its demands on the host, literally absorbing the human body into its workings.

The suggestion of the machine's sentience (that it *decides* to break down, that it is aware and neglectful of Harold's plight, that it responds to the psychological influence of heroin, and so on) is part of the comic effect being employed here. It is an extension of the way we tend to see machines as set apart from other objects in the world because they can act of their own volition (like the human body). The sequence on the road in which Harold leaps out to retrieve the suitcase situates man and machine in distinction to a third category: that of lumpish matter, here represented by the burdensome suitcase, incapable of acting of itself. The domination of matter (of nature) is habitually considered the triumph of the man-machine symbiosis; here the obstinacy of matter and the relentlessness of the machine leave Harold doing all the legwork, struggling to reconcile the two. Relations between man, machine and matter have already been depicted, delightfully, in an earlier moment in the garage that anticipates the rhythm and much of the substance of the later sequence on the road. Ready to set off, Harold hangs his hat and jacket on the wall and goes to turn the engine starter crank; surprisingly, no physical exertion is required — a single twist and already running, his faithful friend. Harold grabs his hat and jacket and springs into the driver's seat, ready to go. The film cuts to a frontal shot from outside the garage, where the right-hand garage door swings halfway shut. Harold climbs out of the car and pushes the door fully open again. No sooner is he back inside the vehicle than the blasted door swings shut again. He clambers out once more, ties it to the fence to keep it open, and gets back in the car, finally ready to go. Whereupon the *left* garage door swings halfway shut. All the while the Ford gently shakes, side to side, with the rhythm of its motor, its convulsions seeming more and more like the mischievous chuckling of a conspirator. Having finally secured both doors and climbed back into the car, Harold is really, actually, finally ready to go. He sticks it into gear and the car lurches backwards, crashing through the back of the garage. It is as if machine and matter were mysteriously colluding against him, alternately imbuing his body with the passivity of the object and the repetitious rhythm of the machine.

If comic effects can result from the machine's playful refusal to accommodate human design, Keaton demonstrates how a positive harmony between man and machine can be equally conducive to comedy. In *The General* (1927), Keaton's hero must act in unison with the steam locomotive along a long stretch of track in order to rescue his train and his girl from enemy soldiers. The train's strength is allied with his ingenuity, its speed with his dexterity. On several occasions his attention is so focused on sustaining the forward momentum of the train — say, in chopping wood for the furnace, or throwing dust under its spinning

4. Body and Machine: A Wrench in the Works

Buster Keaton at one with the machine in *The General* (1927).

wheels to help them engage with the rail — that the wider world slips by unnoticed (as in the first instance) or that he fails to notice that the machine is taking off without him (as in the second). Both Buster and the train employ a mechanical single-mindedness in relation to the immediate task; both duty-bound, they are very much pointed in the same direction.[3] In an exemplary pose, Keaton at one point stands on the speeding train's cabin roof, straight as an arrow and leaning at an oblique angle into the wind, scouting the horizon with his hand to his brow.

The camera's side-on viewpoint incorporates Keaton's fixed body into the train's profile, forming the apex of an aerodynamic line of trajectory that encompasses the cylindrical frontal steam boiler and the train's upright whistle. The pose is comic because of its precision and the way Keaton's whole body leans forward from the ankles up, robust and impervious to the rush of air. Moments later Keaton must clear the rails of wooden sleepers that the enemy soldiers have deposited on the tracks to halt his progress. Slowing the engine to half-speed, he slides down the cowcatcher onto the rails ahead of the train and tries to clear the first beam from the train's path. As the train approaches from the rear, he manages to haul it free just as the train collects him, taking his feet from under him until he finds himself back on the cowcatcher and struggling to bear the heavy sleeper. Just yards ahead, a second beam lies dangerously slanted on the rails; with the train fast approaching, Keaton heaves the first sleeper over his head and vertically down onto the end of the second beam, catapulting it free just in time. By incorporating the principle of the lever, the act strikes a mechanical note that chimes with the way Keaton's position on the cowcatcher figures him as an extension of the train. But his body is not simply a mindless robotic attachment. Indeed, Keaton's heroism at this moment consists in marrying the aptitudes of a fully conscious human agent with the steadfast virtues of the machine: foresight teamed with fortitude, initiative met with precision, swiftness of thought at pace with the momentum of a crankshaft.

Perhaps the most renowned engagement between man and machine in film comedy — the opening factory sequence in Chaplin's

Modern Times (1936) — presents a rather different relationship, and different attitude towards technology. Indeed, our first view of Charlie tightening bolts on the production line immediately suggests the demands of the machine to be in direct conflict with the demands of the body. As the panels whiz past at an uncomfortable speed for Charlie to perform an identical tweak on each bolt, his limbs tense and lips pursed,

One-track mind: Keaton in heroic pursuit in *The General* (1927).

he steps back from the line for a second or two to scratch his under-arm: a lordly, luxurious scratch, almost a stretch, before resuming his duties further down the line, upsetting the rhythms of his colleagues. The humor of the gesture lies in its relative extravagance in a pressured environment, and in its brief but open defiance in prioritizing the body's demands over those of the machine. All of the numerous factory machines — the conveyer belt Charlie works at, the innumerable dials and switches, the clocking-in apparatus, the observation screens which even dominate the workers' washroom — are shown to be in the service not only of increasing worker productivity, but also of strongly regulating the individual body. Most striking in combining these two functions is the Billows Feeding Machine, a contraption that promises (via a record player that expounds the benefits of the device) to eliminate the wasteful period of the lunch break by feeding employees as they continue to work on the production line. Features include a

Publicity still of Charlie Chaplin in *Modern Times* (1936).

mechanized food shoveller, with a retracting arm that pushes bite-sized pieces of fodder into the worker's mouth, and an automaton soup plate with a compressed air blower: "no breath necessary, no energy required to cool the soup," as the accompanying marketing spiel boasts. The potential chill of the line "no breath necessary" is moderated by the upbeat tone of the sales pitch, but the sense in which the machine is designed to *supplant* the body (those aspects of the body that are not "necessary," that is, to profit-making) is filled out by the film's presentation of the ensuing trial run. With the device wheeled out and Charlie reluctantly elected to the post of human guinea pig, Charlie is tightly interned within a protruding brace, and the camera cuts to a viewpoint just above head level so that the entire lower body — the section designed to carry out the menial, repetitive labor — is obscured by the shiny bulk of the apparatus. Far from rendering the machine an augmentation of the body's powers, the visual arrangement thus

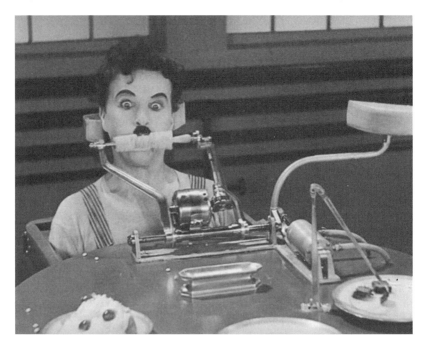

From soup to nuts: Charlie assaulted by the machine in *Modern Times* (1936).

emphasizes the *loss* of the body, its fragmentation and replacement by mechanical procedure.

In severely restricting bodily movement, the feeding machine ensures the body's docility and limits its range of expression. As the automatic mouth-wiping sponge repeatedly forces itself onto his face between courses, the headlocked Charlie can only glare at the offending article in annoyance and disbelief. His eyes become the primary means of expression: flitting between plates in dread at what might be coming next, blinking and squinting when the soup bowl flips tomato broth down his front, wide in terror when attacked by a viciously rotating corncob: enough to assert the persistence of the human through leagues of degradation and the utter incompatibility of body and machine. The machine's interface with the body transforms it into an object, works to reduce the body to its minimal machine-like functions. But Chaplin's eyes assert the body is *not* simply an object to be utilized for economic gain. Importantly — and unlike, say, the bread rolls in *The Gold Rush* or Lloyd's somewhat anthropomorphic car in *Get Out and Get Under*— the machines of *Modern Times* are not invested with human shape or attributes (nor are they portrayed as fantastical monsters like Moloch in Fritz Lang's *Metropolis* [1926]). That would be to divorce industrial machinery from its position in an oppressive work order, as a means of production owned by the bourgeoisie to squeeze profit from the wage laborer. The portrayal of the factory boss (with his omnipresent surveillance and ruthless demands to increase production at any cost) and the acknowledgement of a structured hierarchy along the production line are two ways in which the film ensures that the relation between body and machine is viewed within an industrial-economic context, rather than simply as a phenomenological relation.

It is within such an understanding that *Modern Times* can usefully be seen as a fleshing-out, or comic elaboration, of certain passages of Marx in his damning critique of modern industrialism. The sight of Charlie endlessly tightening bolts on the production line, his eyebrows raised almost haughtily as if waiting for the body's labors to finish, can be seen, for instance, to recall the following passage on worker alienation:

The Body in Hollywood Slapstick

Owing to the extensive use of machinery and to division of labor, the work of the proletarians has lost all individual character, and, consequently, all charm for the workman. He becomes an appendage of the machine, and it is only the most simple, most monotonous, and most easily acquired knack, that is required of him.[4]

The knack required of Charlie to tighten bolts — a sharp little flick of the elbows — becomes a mechanical tick that infects his body even when not on duty, so that in trying to pass a plate of soup to his work colleague, he spasmodically spills the whole lot. As an appendage of the machine, the body loses its elasticity when operating independently: a regular and abrupt twitch might suit the tightening of bolts, but it makes passing a plate of soup a difficult feat indeed.[5] With Charlie's nervous breakdown, the instinct to tighten bolts becomes a fixation. In his deranged balletic rampage around the factory floor, armed with a pair of wrenches, Charlie's mania for bolt tightening leads him to tweak the buttons on women's clothing and even the noses and nipples of his colleagues. His treatment of other bodies as machines here,

An appendage of the machine: Charlie on the production line in *Modern Times* (1936).

4. Body and Machine: A Wrench in the Works

Charlie in the bowels of the machine in *Modern Times* (1936).

exemplified further by the way he cheekily squirts his colleagues with an oilcan, satirizes the manner in which they are already treated by the factory management as mere parts of a larger machine. Consider, for example, the scene following the feeding-machine sequence, in which Charlie strains to keep up with the breakneck rate of the conveyor belt after yet another speed increase has been ordered from on high. The music track underscores the vicious acceleration of the belt with a series of frenzied repeating figures perpetually rising in pitch, while (exploiting the benefits of an independently recorded image track) the camera is cranked at a rate in excess of 24 frames per second to suffuse the bodies onscreen with a maniacal-mechanical motion as they struggle to keep up with its pace. Programmed to serve the requirements of the factory even to the point of self-immolation, Charlie's response to a fumbled bolt is to lunge after it, diving onto the conveyer belt itself and down the chute at the end of the line, sending his body the way of all factory produce in a vivid depiction of Marx's insight that, "exposed to all the vicissitudes of competition, to all the fluctuations of the market," laborers "are themselves a commodity."[6] We next see Charlie being coiled around a series of enormous cogs: the most direct image of the machine *processing* the body, unconscionable to its digestion of human labor. Yet, even here, in the bowels of the factory, Charlie can't refrain from giving the very bolts that help bind him a little tightening tweak.

5

Body and Frame:
Laurel and Hardy

This chapter will make the claim that a major achievement of the films of Laurel and Hardy centers around their exploration of human togetherness, and particularly with regard to the way this is manifested in particular framings of bodies in two of their short films from the 1930s.[1] The pervasive cohesiveness of Laurel and Hardy — reflected in the fact that it is difficult to even think of one without bringing to mind the other — seems to me to be more than a result of their appearing in lots of films together. Rather more precisely, it rests upon the appearance of them *together* (in lots of films). The depths of their togetherness are made most palpable in those moments when the pair are framed together, held together within the same shot, allowing the path of our gaze, moving between one and the other, to trace the lines of their connectedness. The best Laurel and Hardy films draw upon the power of this simple and widely-used cinematic device — the sustained two-shot — to offer a charming, forceful and funny account of what it means for people to *be together.*

In contrast to the sharp dexterity of Chaplin and Keaton, the body in Laurel and Hardy films is typically lumbering, ungainly, clumsy. This clumsiness is frequently manifested in the way Stan and Ollie struggle to complete even the most basic task. In their short film *Busy Bodies* (1933), Stan Laurel and Oliver Hardy are laborers in a joinery workshop, wearing matching denim dungarees and, of course, bowler hats. Stan is energetically planning a piece of wood; Ollie is working on an unfitted window frame. They are working side-by-side along the same workbench but are shown to us separately, each absorbed in his particular task. Ollie finds he can't budge the sliding inner part of the window frame, and applies a mallet to its outer edge, delivering a series of methodical thumps. The sound of Stan's planning continues over shots of Ollie, and the sound of Ollie's thumping can be heard over shots of Stan, so that despite their visual separateness the soundtrack makes us subtly aware of the simultaneity of their actions by means of an uncoordinated percussive duet of thumping and planning. Making no headway with his stubborn window frame, and perhaps becoming a little irritated by the regular and productive sound of Stan's effusive planning, Ollie bangs his mallet three times on the workbench and summons Stan over to help him. Compliantly, Stan puts down his tool and sets about trying to shunt up and down the sliding panes of the window frame, which Ollie stands behind and holds. After a few careful blows of the hammer, Stan manages to heave the window shut — slamming Ollie's fingers and trapping them at the top and bottom of the structure. Failing to register that he has snared Ollie's fingers, Stan twists the central lock, thus securing his colleague's imprisonment, and drifts back offscreen, content with a job well done. Ollie winces through the pane, gazing with practiced disdain at Stan, and then broadly towards the camera in blinking incredulity. His arms spread-eagled across the span of the wooden frame, Ollie ineffectually writhes his torso in attempts to loosen his snared fingers. No good; he summons Stan back over to him and caustically asks if he would mind opening the window. Stan dutifully traipses over into the background of the workshop to let in some fresh air. Ollie's patience snaps and he yells at Stan to help him out. Stan's ensuing attempt to wrestle Ollie free is shown in a series of lengthy frontal two-shots. Finding no joy in operating from outside and in front of the window, Stan then moves around the wooden frame to join Ollie behind the pane. Still having no luck, Stan then squirms underneath Ollie's arm to squeeze himself *between* Ollie and the window. On this movement, we cut to a closer shot of the pair

5. Body and Frame: Laurel and Hardy

Stan Laurel tries to get Oliver Hardy out of trouble in *Busy Bodies* (1933).

in which the sides of the film frame now loosely correspond to the sides of the window frame.

The visual alignment of window frame and film frame, precisely upon the moment at which Stan moves behind the frame to share its tight space with Ollie, implies a correlation between the way their bodies coalesce here and the way their films habitually frame them, together. If this is a self-reflexive gesture, it reads not as willfully artful or knowing, but as a gesture born of an intuitive sense of what is funny about the way these two figures are recurrently bound together by circumstances, friendship and mutual need. As described above, the sequence advances from a presentation of them working separately, albeit side-by-side, to one in which they are brought closer and closer together, advancing from medium-long shots to medium-close-ups, until they are finally squeezed together within the narrow confines of the frame. This movement from separate spaces to shared frame is correspondingly supported by the editing of the sequence. On three occasions in that short sequence, Stan quits his own task and obediently commits himself to helping out his friend (firstly, when he swaggers over to help Ollie shift the wooden panes; secondly, when he again moves to help Ollie open the window; and thirdly, when he moves behind the frame and between Ollie's arms). The repetition of this gesture of commitment is highlighted by a cut on his movement each and every time he saunters over into Ollie's workspace. One result is the humorously repeated emphasis on Ollie's stubborn and then enforced immobility in relation to Stan's patient compliance. Equally important is the way in which *cutting* between Stan's workstation and Ollie's place at the bench works to draw a far sharper line between the two adjacent spaces than, say, *panning* with Stan's movement would have allowed for. The result is an underscoring of the movement from discrete individual locales to a space conspicuous in its sharedness.

This movement from separateness to connectedness (culminating in Stan's movement behind the window frame with Ollie) articulates the wider feeling that Stan and Ollie are somehow, on the one hand, two separate beings each with distinct characteristics, and, on the other hand, a single discrete entity: Laurel-and-Hardy. They are both separate and inseparable. This tension forms the engine of their comedy and the heart of their appeal. Ollie's bossy order for Stan to open the window (and Stan's taking that demand as one for fresh air) evokes something of Ollie's habitual need for Stan's company and his lack of self-sufficiency. The frame frames a picture of Ollie, spread-eagled across its span, helpless without the help of another. Stan's inability to survive without Ollie is perhaps yet more apparent: Stan's strategy of moving inside the frame with Ollie, between his arms, is a childlike expression of *his* neediness. But this proximity allows Stan no leverage, and allows Ollie little room to breathe. It is as if the kind of relationship they embody struggles to find a stable medium between the discomfiture of being apart and the awkwardness of being so close together. On the soundtrack as they struggle within the frame we hear sighs and breaths of exertion, frustration and pain, each giving emphasis — via the ambiguity regarding from which body each noise emanates — to their strenuous physical closeness. The sense of them having become fused — as if awkwardly *sharing* a single body, so tightly are they bound — is attended by the frontal perspective we are offered, which provides a view of the pair in which their identically-dressed bodies overlap.

What better setting for such proceedings than a joinery? — a place where things are welded and hammered and glued together. It is also, of course, a place where things are wrenched and sawn apart, and it is this feature that allows for the film's spectacular resolution of these matters via a huge mechanical bandsaw. Like many of Laurel and Hardy's best films in which they struggle to accomplish a simple task, this environment is also a world of work. The particular environment of *Busy Bodies* bears especial resemblance to that described in Stanley Cavell's following account of Heidegger (which Cavell uses to introduce a brief treatment of the comedy of Buster Keaton):

> In the third chapter of *Being and Time* (the chapter entitled "The World-hood of the World") [Heidegger] makes Being-in-the-World first visible — as a phenomenon for his special analysis — by drawing out, in his way, the implications of our ability to carry on certain simple forms of work, using simple tools in an environment defined by those tools (he calls it a work-world).... It is upon the disturbing or disruption of such carryings on — say by a tool's breaking or by finding something material missing — above all in the disturbing of the kind of perception or absorption that these activities require (something that is at once like attention and like inattention) that, according to Heidegger, a particular form of awareness is called forth.... What this supervening awareness turns out to be *of* is the worldhood of the world.... Heidegger characterizes the supervening awareness as a mode of sight that allows us to see the things of the world in what he calls their conspicuousness, their obtrusiveness, and their obstinacy....[2]

Within the humble perimeters of Laurel and Hardy's world, the disturbing or disruption of their carryings on is a regular comic occurrence.[3] When the window-frame is accidentally refigured as a snare — disturbing the regular rhythms of work — one can hardly fail to notice its obstinacy. Except, of course, the humor of Stan's misinterpretation of Ollie's demand for him to open the window depends upon his failure to see anything out of the ordinary. No supervening awareness appears to overtake Stan; he is still in the same mode of unseeing absorption — "at once like attention and like inattention" — as he was

109

moments earlier when his preoccupation with planning a plank of wood meant that he failed to notice Ollie leaning over the workbench, so tearing a strip of denim from the seat of Ollie's pants. A wonderful feature of this film, by no means uncharacteristic of Stan's behavior, is the way in which his reparation of matters — say, when helping Ollie out of the window frame — is undertaken with the same immersed seriousness and workmanlike concentration he exhibits on the job. Later in the film, Stan diligently endeavors to remove from Ollie's face the remnants of a paintbrush which, in an earlier fit of temper, he had glued to Ollie's chin. His earnest attempts to right the situation, using clamps, pliers and a sharpened plane, constitute loving acts of violence. Taking on the role of barber allows Stan the privilege of depersonalized grooming, applying himself with something like a craftman's pride towards Ollie's body. Stan's pre-philosophical attitude allows us to notice, and invites us to consider, the *physicality* of Ollie's body.

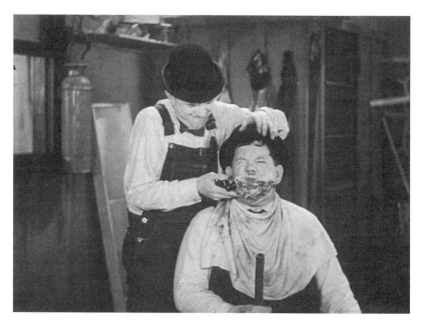

This won't hurt a bit: Stan shaves Ollie with a workman's plane in *Busy Bodies* (1933).

Similarly, with Ollie's fingers ensnared in the window frame, our attention as viewers is given over to the *obstinate* friction of wood on wood; to the *conspicuousness* of the way windows slam shut as well as open to let in fresh air; to the awkward *obtrusiveness* of fingers rather than their utility.

The escalation of problems in the window-frame sequence is quite characteristic of a certain tendency in Laurel and Hardy's films in which, as Gilberto Perez notes, "things can be counted on to get madly out of control."[4] The small problem of how to close a window frame leads, by means of its solution, to the larger predicament of how to yank Ollie's hands free from that closed frame; the solution to *that* problem will involve Stan launching himself onto Ollie from the top of the workbench and the pair crashing down onto a passing work colleague, instigating a petty conflict with that now-hostile workmate and so initiating *another* fine mess. This familiar pattern constitutes an important factor in creating a sense of comic anticipation, but it also

Framed: Ollie with his fingers stuck in *Busy Bodies* (1933).

111

feeds into a deeper understanding of the comedy of Laurel and Hardy, one which responds to the happy, fateful inexorability of their coming-together-again. Frequently, Laurel and Hardy's 1930s short films begin with Stan and Ollie in separate spaces — say, with the pair looking for one another at a train station, or with Ollie asking Stan to come over and help clean his house, or with Stan setting out to visit Ollie in hospital — in a manner that points forward towards their inevitable convergence. This structure of coming-together (and moving apart in order to come-together-again) is then replayed over and over, with nuance and variety, at the level of editing and mise-en-scene, as in the sequence described above. Held apart in separate and alternated shots, events conspire to bring the pair together — back together — within the same frame. In this regard, the short comedies of Laurel and Hardy share some territory with the genre of remarriage comedy as described by Stanley Cavell, of which he notes as a dominant concern the drive to bring the central couple *"back* together, together *again."*[5] Cavell also offers the following description (principally about the central couple of *It Happened One Night* [1934]) which chimes with a certain appreciation of Laurel and Hardy:

> What this pair does together is less important than the fact that they do whatever it is together, that they know how to spend time together, even that they would rather waste time together than do anything else — except that no time they are together could be wasted. Here is a reason these relationships strike us as having the quality of friendship....[6]

We might say — not merely on account of the fact that Laurel and Hardy tend to share the same double bed, portion out domestic chores and live in each other's pockets — that Stan and Ollie's friendship strikes us as having something of the quality of marriage, where that condition is characterized, as Cavell characterizes it, as requiring "a willingness for repetition, the willingness for remarriage."[7] The drive to bring Stan and Ollie *"back* together, together *again"* manifests itself at the level of framing, editing and staging to present their repeated reconvergence as something in-between an active pursuit of togetherness and a passive surrender to a mysterious magnetism.

This pattern of habitual "remarriage" forms the rhythmic and

"Fresh fish!": Stan and Ollie as budding entrepreneurs in *Towed in a Hole* (1932).

thematic basis of one of their finest short films, *Towed in a Hole* (1932), in which Stan and Ollie, as budding fresh fish salesmen, undertake to renovate a boat so they can use it to catch fish. The narrative of this film is thus concerned with how this pair can construct a space wherein they can more fruitfully be together. Of course, in the event, the boat never becomes seaworthy; a central joy of this film is the way the process of scrubbing, squabbling, pushing and painting turns out to be more important than the accomplishment of its ostensible goal. The film is built around the repeated reconvergence of the couple within and around the space of the boat. Early on in the film, Stan is scrubbing the deck, while Ollie is down below painting the boat's rudder. They are in separate spaces, shown in separate shots, and each is absorbed in his own separate task. Ollie sits on a little stool beside the rudder with a paint-pot between his knees; Stan seeks to clear the deck for scrubbing, so he shoves the rudder-lever to the right, out of his way.

Of course, down below, the rudder swings left, Ollie is tipped off his stool and the paint pot ends up on his head. Stan carries on with the scrubbing, oblivious to the consequence of his action. The subsequent appearance of Ollie's head over the side of the boat, paint now plastered all over his face, warrants a double-take from Stan and a guilty, if baffled, withdrawal. He retreats from Ollie's prickly stare over the edge of the boat so that only his eyes and hat are visible; when Ollie angrily clambers up onto the deck, Stan slowly circles around the hull, glancing up at Ollie with the facial mannerisms of a quizzical seagull. The film's strategy of editing matches Stan's deferral of the inevitable confrontation; in its commitment to framing each of the pair separately as Stan circles around the boat, the film achieves a humorous delay and anticipation of their unavoidable coming-together.

We are rewarded with a bucket-and-hose routine displayed in an almost unbroken single take lasting the best part of three glorious minutes. The setting of this tit-for-tat squabble on the deck of the boat, along the camera's angle-of-view, allows the boat's mast in the background to run right down the middle of the screen and between the pair so as to create a framing that evokes a loose symmetry. At the same time, the disparate physiognomies of wiry-thin Stan and rotund Ollie, on each side of the visual divide, evoke a sense of disequilibrium. The paradoxical impression of symmetry *and* disequilibrium achieved in setting these bodies in this frame in this way — an evocation of the very phrase "tit-for-tat" — heralds the unbalanced escalation about to take place under the guise of equal-and-opposite reactions.

Ollie tips a bucket of water over Stan; Stan does the same in return. Ollie laboriously positions a stick to hold open the top of Stan's dungarees, careful not to spill the water he holds in a bucket, before slowly and meticulously tipping it down inside. Stan's response shifts from puzzled detachment to passive acceptance to mild admiration as Ollie finishes pouring, before chivalrously signaling to the perpetrator that he has not yet received his full due: the bucket is not quite empty. It is only proper, it seems, that he should receive a punishment equal to the bucket of water he tipped over Ollie: exactly a bucketful, no more, no less. Ollie's scrupulous care in finishing off the job finds its

Tit for tat: Stan hoses down Ollie's behind, so Ollie pours water into Stan's dungarees. *Towed in a Hole* (1932).

complement — after Stan has waited patiently for his turn and Ollie has naively bent over to pick something up — in the workmanlike efficiency with which Stan then hoses Ollie's fat rump: tuning the hose-nozzle down to form a narrower blast of water, observing with satisfaction the targeted surface area as if spraying the side of a bus. The camera's patience and frontal view mirrors the ritualistic restraint of this mannerly exchange of buckets and hose-jets of water, setting in ironic relief the way each gesture of petty revenge raises the stakes a little further. As things start to spiral out of control, Ollie calls a truce to take the moral high ground: "This is why we never get any place," he announces. Then, slowly and firmly, hand on hip, pompously lingering upon each consonant:

United we stand ... Divided we fall.

Ollie's oratorical pose, his left hand thrust skywards with an up-stretched finger, ostentatiously resembles that of the Statue of Liberty, and this is as explicit a Declaration of Interdependence as can be found in the films of Laurel and Hardy. The truth of the latter part of Ollie's platitude is ironically confirmed in the mishap that ensues. Blinded by his haughty principles, Ollie swaggers towards the camera and out of the frame (leaving Stan alone to rue his actions) — only to slip on a bar of soap, skim across the deck and careen headfirst overboard into a puddle of spilled paint. Rather than showcasing Ollie's acrobatics in a long shot, the succession of quick cuts that detail the fall (foot slipping leftwards, Ollie soaring rightwards, paint flying left to splash on wood, Ollie face down in the puddle) vigorously chops up the space, in stark contrast to the long-take presentation of the preceding bucket-and-hose sequence, so accentuating the feeling of sudden division.

They seem somehow unable to remain apart for very long. Moments later, Ollie is nailing patches of wood to the side of the boat to stop leaks (the cabin is filled with water) while Stan is on deck scrubbing the anchor clean. Once again the film lays stress on their separateness by crosscutting between one-shots of each privately absorbed in separate tasks. In a characteristic moment of thoughtlessness, Stan hastily dispatches the anchor over the edge of the cabin roof and instinc-

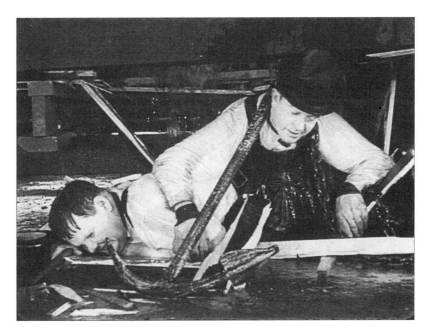

Another fine mess: Stan and Ollie beneath the hulk in *Towed in a Hole* (1932).

tively grips the anchor chain—it yanks him over and down with a crash, right through the belly of the boat. The hard cut to ground-level shows Ollie and Stan now lumped together and water spewing out of the hulk; Stan is strewn over Ollie's rump and held there by the anchor chain around his neck. The suddenness of this cut—from a flurry of movement to a static, composed image—lends a magical effect to their confluence, accentuated by the fact that we don't see the landing. It is difficult to imagine exactly how these bodies could have ended up quite so pictorially contorted, wrapped up together under the boat.

As with the window-frame sequence earlier, we are offered here an image of too-tight proximity. This fusion of bodies is a recurrent source of hilarity in Laurel and Hardy. A telling example of this phenomenon is the sequence in *Berth Marks* (1929) in which Stan and Ollie, on an overnight train, endeavor to change into nightwear while sharing a cramped sleeping berth. A lengthy take presents the pair squashed up together with each trying in vain to execute the broad physical maneuvers necessary to remove their jackets, trousers and shirts. Ollie labors to heave one half of his elastic braces off his shoulder, but it ends up round Stan's neck; meanwhile, Stan is occupied in trying to wriggle out of his waistcoat, one side of which gets hooked over Ollie's head. The dialogue of the scene, muttered and barked in hot-headed frustration, parallels this fusion, and confusion, of bodies:

OLLIE: Would you not crowd me so much?!
Get your head off of mine!
STAN: Hey, you're choking me here.
OLLIE: Don't crowd so much!
STAN: Don't keep pushing me like that.
OLLIE: You're choking me!
Get your foot out of my face! And don't crowd.
Stay on your own side.
Would you stop crowding?!
Get that thing off my foot, and give it to me.
Did you know that you have my pants on your leg?

Cast in all their clumsy, breathy physicality, these two bodies struggle to remain discrete. The resort to language here, and to bossy orders in particular, at least allows the use of "me/my" and "you/your" to suggest some kind of distinction; but the fact that they choose to sleep in a single berth already suggests an unwillingness to be isolated from one another. Encapsulated here, and in the other examples I have discussed, is the central comic, perhaps existential, problem of Laurel and Hardy. They struggle to settle a balanced existence with one another, but seem unable to exist apart.

How might the demand for separateness achieve reconciliation with the need for togetherness? Frequently, as is the case with *Towed in a Hole*, these films end with a chase into the distance, with a blubbing Stan galloping away from a fuming Ollie, hand on hat, in hot pursuit. Such endings strike a definitive note of continuation: things will carry on in this vein, out of sight and beyond the end of this particular narrative (like "they lived happily ever after" but set in something more like the present or future tense). That these endings do feel like endings suggests that Stan and Ollie exist in a stable state of perpetual instability. We noticed earlier that the visual arrangement and measured give-and-take procedure of their escalating water fight somehow evoked a sense of balance-in-disequilibrium. (Somehow descriptions of Laurel and Hardy seem to gravitate towards oxymoron — complementary contrariness, perhaps, or harmonious dissonance — a feature perhaps most strongly deriving from the appearance of their dissimilar bodies clothed in identical attire.) Both the tit-for-tat squabble and the concluding chase allow for the pair to function both as a single consolidated unit (bickering among themselves or sprinting into the distance) *and* as two discrete and reciprocal entities (subject/object; chaser/chased).

Something like this is declared in the final shot of *Towed in a Hole*. In this last scene of the film, the pair discover that their little Model T Ford can't muster the power to tow their newly-restored fishing boat down the hill, even with Ollie's attempts to shove it, and Stan helpfully suggests that Ollie puts the sails up (a neat instance here of Ollie acting as *body* and Stan, ironically, as *mind*). Ollie delicately licks his finger and holds it aloft between the pair of them. He holds it there for a second to feel the breath of the wind, while Stan *looks* at it, musingly, before the pair glance at one another and simultaneously nod in satisfied agreement (as if they even share the sense-perception of touch!). Unfortunately, calamity strikes when, the sails having been raised, the boat lurches down the hill and crashes into the car. In the film's final shot, Ollie lurches after Stan, chasing him past the collision wreckage, a muddled amalgamation of boat and car. We might notice the visual/metaphorical resemblances between Ollie and the large cumbersome boat, on the one hand, and between Stan and the gawky little car, on the other. We might also notice the way in which this pile-up rhymes with the earlier collision between Stan and Ollie when Stan fell through the hulk of the boat. As Ollie chases Stan and the film fades out, we are left with an image of their fusion and of their distinctness.

As with so many other Laurel and Hardy shorts, *Busy Bodies* also culminates in the destruction of Stan and Ollie's Model T Ford. Fleeing the worksite where they have managed to flatten a shed on their boss, the pair hurriedly clamber into their car and drive straight into

Stan and Ollie's car gets sawn in half in *Busy Bodies* (1932).

another barn, where a six-foot bandsaw awaits to wreak its damage. The spinning blade scythes through the bonnet and, as a confounded Stan and Ollie turn to watch its path, it continues to plough *right between the two of them*, sawing their automobile in half. With the bandsaw having traversed the whole length of the vehicle, Stan and Ollie wobble and teeter in their separate chunks of car, each precariously balanced on two wheels for just a few seconds, before finally falling to either side with a crash.

The series of camera positions from which we view this scene of wreckage stresses the violent tearing apart of the couple. As the bandsaw begins to rip through the bonnet, a medium long-shot presents the devastation in profile such that their bodies are as close as possible to one another in the frame. Dressed in identical clothes and with no clear line of distinction between them, Stan and Ollie share a single outline. By contrast, once the saw has passed the full length of the car, the film cuts to a series of frontal shots which serve to accentuate the

5. Body and Frame: Laurel and Hardy

Two's company: Laurel and Hardy in an exemplary pose for *Towed in a Hole* (1932).

distance between Stan and Ollie as they consecutively crash down. Each fall, when it comes, is pictured in a separate two-shot, the first framed to favor Stan as he subsides to the extreme left of the frame, the second to favor Ollie as he collapses to its extreme right. Significantly, however, the action is precisely arranged so that neither Stan nor Ollie *quite* disappears off-screen as they tumble towards its edge. The frame holds these bodies together in an invisible embrace.

What is stressed here is the continuation of the couple — as in concert they pull themselves to their feet, specked with sawdust, adjusting their bowlers in bemusement — beyond the threat of their severance. It takes the *deus ex machina* of the bandsaw to separate them — by splicing in two the car which had earlier held them within its narrow breadth on their journey to work — but the use of framing still sustains them as a couple, as if to insist on their ability to carry on together whatever happens. The use of the two-shot can become significant in

121

this way because of the weight repeatedly placed on the nuanced inter-action between Stan and Ollie within a single sustained frame. The bucket-and-hose sequence from *Towed in a Hole* and the window-frame sequence from *Busy Bodies* are two such notable occasions, gain-ing their significance from the broader context of the patterns and structure of the film, and from the manner in which they are arrived at and departed from. The films are built around the coming-together-again of the central couple, within the same space, and within the same frame. While we might say that Stan and Ollie are always in some sense together even when not sharing the same space, these films place weight on the *physical* dimension of togetherness, stressing the fact that being-together is very much an *embodied* experience. Such an account allows the comedy of Laurel and Hardy to counterpoise the awkwardness, annoyances and complications thrown up by physical proximity against the necessity, value and joy of companionship.

6

Body and Voice: Physical and Verbal Comedy

How does physical comedy incorporate the voice? The Marx Brothers might be thought to represent, in the figures of the mute Harpo and the ever-wisecracking Groucho, two extremes of physical and verbal humor respectively, and to register as a result an underlying tension between body and voice. While Groucho's distinctive vocal delivery — with its relentless tone and tempo, dispensing insults and commentary with an acerbic wit — might be thought to constitute the rhythmic backbone of Marx Brothers comedy, a kind of counterpoint is provided by Harpo's mute eruptions of ecstasy, rage, madness or unbridled joy. While we might detect a centripetal tendency in Groucho's quickfire remarks — drawing in the surrounding world towards a central ego — Harpo's anarchic physicality acts as a centrifugal force, allowing disorder to emanate from his body and randomly disturb the bureaucratic world around him. While the voice is the nucleus of Groucho's identity, Harpo *is* his body: declaring as much in a moment from *Duck Soup* (1933), when Groucho asks him, "Say, who are you, anyway?" and Harpo replies by showing a picture of his own face, tattooed onto his own arm. He must get asked that question a lot.

The centrality of the voice in Groucho's performance is affirmed in a moment from *A Day at the Races* (1937) when (while Groucho is distracted by an argument with Chico) Harpo furtively injects Grou-

Barrel of laughs: Groucho Marx, the fastest mouth in the west.

cho's leg with Novocaine. The possibilities for extended slapstick offered by this situation are passed up, however; instead, the comedy takes the form of a neat verbal quip, with Groucho uttering, "I hate to admit it, but I haven't got a leg to stand on," before shuffling out of the room. While Groucho's body is typified by this kind of inflexibility, even at the best of times (one thinks of his stiff-backed pacing, the

indelible-ink moustache and that mechanical roll of his eyes upon a punchline), his *voice* is distinguished by a supple responsiveness, knowing and immediate, perpetually picking up on an innocuous phrase and twisting it into a pun or double entendre. Conversely, it is Harpo's *body* that is so sharply reactive to the world around him — hanging his leg, where he can, on someone else's momentarily extended hand — while his voice is inflexibly silent. A good example of these conflicting ten-

Silent clown: Harpo Marx looking disconcertingly demure.

6. Body and Voice: Physical and Verbal Comedy

Harpo Marx tears through customs control in *Monkey Business* (1931).

dencies of body and voice is the sequence in *Monkey Business* (1931) where the Brothers are trying to make their way through customs control, but the only passport they have between them has been pinched from the pocket of Maurice Chevalier. Consequently, each of them in turn tries to pass himself off as Chevalier by performing "A New Kind of Love" for the customs-officials. As Zeppo, Chico and Groucho push through the assembled queue, sidle up to the officials and impersonate, in turn and with increasing ineptitude, Chevalier's French-accented crooning, the routine hinges on the farcical insistence with which each of the group declares himself to be the unique and genuine article by means of the *same* snatch of a popular song ("If a nightingale / Could sing like you..."), and on a beautifully fuzzy but unswervingly maintained logic that contends that a sufficiently convincing voice would bowl over the officials despite the lack of likeness to the passport photograph: that is, that the voice might supersede the body as the primary token of identity. The officials, unsurprisingly, are not fooled.

125

"Look at that face," the customs officer protests, pointing to the photograph. "Well, look at *that* face," replies Groucho, gesturing to a toffee-nosed lady in the queue behind him.

Presently, Harpo steps up onto the customs-officials' table and parades down the catwalk in his open trenchcoat, gesturing regally as he bypasses the incensed queue. Reaching customs control, he pumps on the passport stamp with his foot as if he were inflating a tyre, and manically pitches piles of official papers into the air. Forcibly withheld around the waist by a bemused officer, he scrambles excitedly around and grabs hold of a pair of pens in their fixed stands, using them like gearsticks or as if he is rowing. The officer demands a passport. Harpo offers pasteboard. "Not pasteboard," yells the officer. "Passport!" Harpo offers a washboard. Voice or no voice, the logic of puns and wordplay permeates even the voiceless illogic of Harpo's behavior. Indeed, such visual-verbal quips trump even the swiftness of Groucho's retorts, the props being as magically ready-to-hand for Harpo as any put-down is for Groucho's barbed tongue. This magical quality of Harpo's physicality seems importantly related to his muteness, which marks him out as essentially belonging to a different realm than that of the speaking characters (the realm of the imaginary, perhaps, rather than that of the symbolic).[1]

Finally producing Maurice Chevalier's ID, Harpo's impersonation (made even more tricky by his obstinate muteness) is aided by a wind-up gramophone, strapped to his back and playing the Chevalier record, to which he accordingly lip-synchs with a feverish grin. As the record winds down, distorting Chevalier's voice and hampering Harpo's deception, the game is up; the officer lurches to grab the gramophone, and Harpo returns to hurling around official documents, securing the officer in a headlock and repeatedly rubber-stamping his bald head. The movement from broad physical comedy (parading down the table, hurling papers) to a type of comedy obliquely based on wordplay and voice (the punning props, lip-synching to Chevalier), and back again to an anarchic comedy of the body, is correspondingly registered by a shift in the camera's proximity to the action, cutting from medium-long-shot to medium-shot for the duration of Harpo's exchange with the officer. In fact, with the strapped-on gramophone curtailing his physical movement — Harpo must remain frontal to the officer to hide the contraption, and he has to wind it up behind his back — and with his aping of conventional romantic crooning gestures, Harpo's temporary acquisition of a voice is presented as *inhibiting* a physicality that is otherwise boisterous, unruly and self-possessed. Groucho, on the other hand, manages to channel these same qualities into comebacks and quips — but then he has quite a way with words.

The sequence as a whole comically presents a dualistic idea of the relation between voice and body. The impression of a voice/body disjunction is heightened by the lyrics of "A New Kind of Love," which offers the strange mental image of a nightingale singing sweetly with a human voice. In addition, the final "...to me!" of the chorus, which Harpo silently mouths with an overblown clasping of his heart, highlights the discrepancy between the "Me" that sings and the "Me" that effusively gestures. With the bizarre assamblage of Chevaliers's recorded voice and Harpo's body, the sequence cheekily draws attention to an ontological condition of the talking picture: that sound and image tracks are joined together in a more or less successful illusion of a synchronous and homogenous whole. As Michel Chion notes:

> The sound film, for its part, is dualistic. Its dualism is hidden or disavowed to varying extents; sometimes cinema's split is even on display. The physical nature of film necessarily makes an incision or cut between the body and the voice. Then the cinema does its best to restitch the two together at the seam.[2]

However, for Chion, this project of restitching to achieve the outcome of synchronous dialogue has the consequential effect of privileging the voice over the body:

> The spoken utterance, which conveys words, emotions, or a message, makes all the more apparent the *cinema's diversion of attention from the "whole" human being to just its voice*, the absence of the body from what the mouth is saying, the voice's very denial of the body.[3]

If physical comedy, as we have seen, involves itself in a forceful declaration of the body, slapstick seems antithetical to the "spoken utterance" as outlined by Chion. This may go some way to explaining

why silent film has been historically more conducive to slapstick comedy than the sound cinema. Performers as diverse as Groucho Marx,
Mae West, Bob Hope and Woody Allen can be found in different ways
to deny or de-emphasize the body. Groucho's utterance of "I haven't
got a leg to stand on" is a rare moment in which he comments on his
body, but even here the emphasis is very much on wordplay over horseplay. Mae West may be flagrantly sensual in her bodily presence, but
her witty commentary and unbroken innuendo represent the core of
her comedy, and in fact work to keep sexual encounter as a reference
point, cloaked from view. The cynical remarks of Bob Hope sustain
him at an authoritative distance from the world, where mishaps of the
body can always be redeemed by a droll aside. Woody Allen's musings
knowingly seek to compensate for an inadequate physicality, for a body
that is apt to betray you at a crucial moment, say by sneezing into a
bag of cocaine.[4] Indeed, it is Woody Allen's comedy, a comedy of the
spoken utterance bar none, that might most clearly exemplify that
duality of body and voice that Chion sees as inherent to the sound film.
His variety of intellectual humor separates the mind from the body by
allying the voice to the mind. This dichotomy provides the very structure of *Sleeper* (1973), for instance, which alternates between sequences
of dry, verbal humor sustained by the rhythm of Allen's one-liners, and
sequences of broad physical comedy (clearly paying deliberate homage
to Chaplin, Keaton, the Marx Brothers and Mack Sennett). The line
between the two styles is sharply drawn: the slapstick sequences are primarily filmed in long-shot, often set outside, and accompanied by hectic Dixieland jazz — which halts abruptly at the end of a sequence,
holding these scenes of anarchic physicality firmly apart from scenes
of verbal wit. The film duplicates this dichotomy in a series of presentations of unlikely matches between body and voice: in one dreamlike
sequence, Allen performs an extended vocal impersonation of Vivien
Leigh's Blanche DuBois; in another, after expounding an intellectual
position, he is crowned the unlikely winner of a Miss USA competition. Against the sterility of a futuristic world that consigns sexuality
to an Orgasmatron machine and seeks to control the body through
cloning procedures, the sequences of physical comedy offer a chaotic

and lively alternative vision. Yet it is the voice, not the body, that provides the principal medium both for Allen's philosophical ruminations and for comedic showmanship.

Are physical and verbal comedy fundamentally at odds?— the former by affirming the body while the latter denies it? No less a figure than Charlie Chaplin was skeptical of their integration. In an essay published in the *New York Times* in 1931, Chaplin justified his famous refusal to produce talking pictures even as the rest of Hollywood seemed reconciled to the change. "Silent comedy is more satisfactory entertainment for the masses than talking comedy," he argued, "because most comedy depends on swiftness of action, and an event can happen and be laughed at before it can be told in words."[5] However flawed as an indictment of talkies (which rarely tell an event in words if the event is worth showing), Chaplin's words seem an apt justification of his wish to avoid dialogue in his films; for the very finest of Chaplin's achievements — *The Cure* (1917), *The Adventurer* (1917), *The Idle Class* (1921), *The Kid* (1921), *Payday* (1922), *The Pilgrim* (1923), *The Gold Rush* (1925), much of *Modern Times* (1936)— crucially depend on this "swiftness of action," the thrill of trying to keep up with Charlie's every move, the majestic fluency of the body in motion, heightened by its noiselessness.

Chaplin's best comedy champions the body as it champions the voiceless underdog. In a celebrated scene from a silent Chaplin film, *The Pilgrim*, Chaplin plays an escaped convict disguised as a pastor who is shepherded into a rural church to deliver a bible sermon. Charlie's improvised response is to act out David and Goliath, and he goes about it with energy and aplomb. First he demonstrates the size and stature of Goliath by indicating a great height, clasping his biceps and miming the important detail, unmentioned in the Bible account, of Goliath's colossal moustache. Now for David: he is small (about a foot high), but when Goliath picks on him, David won't stand for it, pointing and hollering back up at him (no doubt some well-deserved obscenity). But Goliath waves his big old sword around, so David picks up a stone and hurls it at him. Charlie mimes the devastating result in gruesome detail: the stone goes right into Goliath's forehead and right out the other side (fancy that!); David counts him out, wrestling-style, and

Mime, all mime: Chaplin preaches in *The Pilgrim* (1923).

chops off his head; he then holds it aloft and back-kicks it out of sight. The sermon doesn't go down too well with the congregation (except for one small boy who energetically applauds this break from the usual stuffy nonsense, under protest from his mother). But Charlie, ever the consummate professional, takes a stage bow and gaily skips off, coming back for a second, third, even fourth round of adulation despite the reticence of the crowd. Charlie's sermon is vigorously *physical*: a hearty intervention of the physical in the realm of the spiritual, like a gust of fresh air blowing the Sunday hats off the pious lady worshippers. The congregation are stunned, not just by the crudeness of the sermon, but by the vitality of the body, turning emblem and allegory into flesh and blood and guts.

Such an effect is achievable because there is no possibility, hence no requirement, that Charlie should speak.[6] In a sound film, such effusive miming would have looked like dumb-play, and the speaking voice is surely too keen an indicator of status and authority for the con-

6. Body and Voice: Physical and Verbal Comedy

Only the voice of Hynkel was heard: Charlie Chaplin in *The Great Dictator* (1940).

vict to have plausibly carried off the social fraud. Indeed, in Chaplin's post-transition films of the 1930s (each of which uses a synchronized soundtrack, but no dialogue as such), the relation between speech and authority is boldly outlined. Intermittent sequences in both *City Lights* (1931) and *Modern Times* allow those with power — city governors and factory boss, respectively — to speak. At the start of *City Lights*, the pomposity of city governors delivering speeches at a public ceremony is sent up by the use of squealing trumpets in place of human voices. The device works wonderfully to mimic the all-important *tone* of public oration; but the governors still have a voice of sorts, and a platform. In *Modern Times*, the factory boss appears on a videoscreen in the toilets where Charlie is trying to smoke a quick cigarette in his break. "Hey! Quit stalling! Get back to work!" barks the Boss, and Charlie has no response but to toddle off back to the production line. In Chaplin's first dialogue picture, *The Great Dictator* (1940), the alliance

131

between voice and authority is even more pronounced, and employed for satirical effect. In the early sequence in which the mad tyrant Hynkel (an undisguised caricature of Adolf Hitler) addresses the nation at a fascist rally, Chaplin's comic use of Germanic gibberish (*"eh der Strat mit Hupensecht, der Wiener-Schnitzel mit der Lager weden und der Sauerkraut!"*) effectively sends up the lunacy and the viciousness of the despot through the medium of voice, lampooning fascism's excessively rhetorical style of oration and pointing up the division of language from sense. An English "translation" (spoken in voiceover, newsreel-style) humorously highlights the Dictator's verbosity by condensing minutes of ferocious gabble into a succinct one-line summary: "Yesterday Tomainia was down but today she has risen." As a denunciation of wordiness, as much as a condemnation of fascism, this vocal strategy is pithy and sharp. Meanwhile, the Dictator's hateful utterances are shown to emerge as bodily excretions: most notably, when Hynkel curses the Jews and a standing microphone bends away from his spittle as if in response to the repugnancy of his meaning, and, at another moment, when Hynkel's vociferous barking literally disintegrates into a coughing fit, sustaining the rhythm and guttural tone of the speech, not so much interrupting the speech as continuing it. For all its vigor and venom, the Dictator's oratorical bombast is shown up for what it really is: a load of phlegm and spittle.

Yet the highlight of the film is Chaplin's juxtaposition of two wonderful, wordless scenes of physical comedy: the Dictator's power-giddy dance with his globe, and the Barber's shaving of a customer to the rhythm of Brahms' Hungarian Dance No.5 (issuing from the radio). The former is an absurd and beautiful ballet that humorously characterizes the Dictator's wild thirst for world domination with the controlled and effeminate manner of a trained dancer. With balance and poise, the Dictator approaches the globe, hands on hips, like a gymnast in repose. He lifts it with fingertips (it turns out to be inflatable) and proficiently spins the globe on one digit, letting out a fiendish cackle as the camera gracefully withdraws. The latter sequence, which follows directly, is a succinct demonstration of the way one's everyday, unreflexive comportment can be unknowingly influenced by external

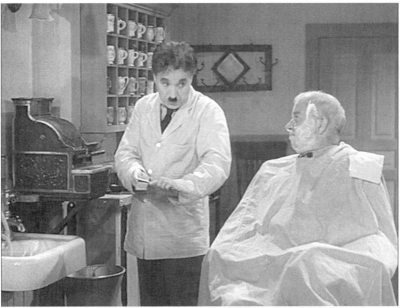

The delicacy in the Dictator (top), the brutality in the Barber...: *The Great Dictator* (1940).

forces, to the extent that the simple act of shaving to music can appear to contain murderous intent. With the customer seated and daubed with shaving cream, the Barber sharpens his blade to a *legato* strain that anticipates the re-emergence of the song's violent central motif, the calm before the storm. He raises his eyebrows as he fiendishly sways to the strings, ominously cocking an eye at the man in the chair before returning to his sharpening; and as the music jolts back into its vigorous rhythm, he briskly plucks a hair from his own head, runs it through the blade, and moves to circle his helpless target. Chaplin's incisive use of the body draws *parallels* between the characters, beyond their merely sharing the same moustache, to reveal the potential for good and evil in *both* men: the delicacy in the Dictator, we might say, and the brutality in the Barber. These two scenes amply justify Chaplin's suspicion of dialogue by showing how expressive wordlessness can be.[7]

In sharp contrast to Chaplin's reluctance to produce talkies is the apparent ease with which Laurel and Hardy made the transition to

Ssshhhh! Laurel and Hardy's comedy made a favorable transition to sound.

sound. Even their silent shorts make full use of the comic potential of sound, often calling for quite a level of sophistication on the part of the live musical accompaniment (the extended bandstand sequence in *You're Darn Tootin'* (1929), for instance, as Stan and Ollie interject and misplay musical phrases, drop their instruments and fall off seats, requires a sensitive and alert matching of sound to silent image).[8] With a synchronized soundtrack, the addition of lifelike sound effects — of pianos crashing down stairs and vases being smashed on craniums — plays a vital role in fleshing out the physicality of this most physical of film worlds. Sound offers a more full-bodied sensory experience of Stan and Ollie's frustrated endeavors by allowing us vividly to *hear*, as well as to see, how one physical mass encounters another (such as a pie in the face), or how an object falls apart — and to hear, as well as to see, the embellished reactions of Stan and Ollie to their mishaps, frequently characterized by whoops of alarm, yells of pain or grunts of displeasure (such as Ollie's exasperated refrain of "Hm-mm-*mmmm!*"). Moreover, whereas the demand for stars to speak reputedly cut short many performers' careers (such as that of Buster Keaton, whose voice was heard to jar with his visual persona), the addition of voices extends and deepens the characters of Stan and Ollie. Oliver Hardy's big-barrel chest turned out to produce a suitably strident speaking voice, capable of rasping bossy instructions with a baritone mock-authority. Meanwhile, Stan Laurel's unadorned northern–English accent was apt to convey a childlike ingenuousness, ranging across the scale from disgruntled murmuring and generally cheerful pronouncements at the low end, sliding up to shrill and squeaky blubbing when threatened with punishment (face screwed up, mouth widened, eyes narrowed to hold back tears). In this way, their voices extend the humorous impression of a relationship between a pompous parent and a befuddled child. But just as their contrasting bodies unite them in clumsiness and mishap, their contrasting voices echo and mimic one another in tone and substance. When Ollie is out of commission with a broken leg in *County Hospital* (1932) and Stan brings along the gift of some unshelled eggs and brazil nuts, Ollie's irritation is voiced only through a sullen, growling repetition, delivered to camera: *"Hard-boiled eggs and nuts...."* By

135

forsaking a witty or cathartic punchline, and instead echoing Stan's cheery announcement of his bedside gift, the response humorously reiterates Ollie's thorough lack of autonomy, his incapacity to rise above the cause of his frustration. A similar echoing can be heard in the following exchange from *Sons of the Desert* (1933). Stan and Ollie are hiding in the attic from their wives, and Stan has just climbed into bed with Ollie:

STAN: "We're just like two peas in a pot."
OLLIE: "Not pot. Pod-*duh*. Pod-*duh*."
STAN: (turning out the light, lying down, and after a pause) "Pod-*duh*."

The fastidiousness of Ollie's instruction is underscored by his hand movement which curls upwards from his mouth, as if to indicate the passage of the tongue across the palate required to make the *duh* sound; a good example of the way gesture is used to complement dialogue. This exchange in the attic is a relatively quiet respite from the slapstick antics that precede and follow it, but it nonetheless contains much of what is at the core of Laurel and Hardy's most broad and physical comedy: simple repetitions; sameness and difference; Ollie's superiority; Stan's literal-mindedness; the two of them together like two peas in a pod-*duh*. In this way, forgoing the opportunities afforded by sound technology to add witty one-liners or sophisticated banter to their comic routines, Laurel and Hardy use dialogue to underpin, rather than subsume, the achievements of their physical comedy.

A similarly favorable transition from silent to sound cinema was made by W.C. Fields. In fact, it may be said that no comic figure depends more on the expressiveness of the voice: on the relation between what is said and how it is said. "Listen: you've all gotta realize one thing," he tells his daughter in *It's a Gift* (1934), muting his voice lest his wife in the next room should hear. "That *I* "—venturing to raise his voice for a second, with a quick glance around, before returning to a mutter—"am the master of this household." Meanwhile, his body language confirms what his tone of voice betrays. His side-of-the-mouth expression and slightly rolling head movement strive to communicate a confident masculine resolve, but they spring from a need to *contain* the

6. Body and Voice: Physical and Verbal Comedy

"I ... am the master of this household": W.C. Fields with Jean Rouverol in *It's a Gift* (1933).

volume of his voice for fear of being contradicted. His hand gestures are clumsily inhibited, with a brief and limp wag of his finger when he asserts his "I," and a tellingly guarded thumb-point in the direction of the missus when he utters the word "household"—upon which a shrill voice from the adjacent room calls "Harold!" and his fingers nervously leap to his hat brim. The moment rounds off an opening sequence that has been built around the competing demands of family members: to shave, to skate, to smoke, to eat, to speak. Harold tries to shave while his daughter applies make-up; she manages to obtain the bathroom mirror and Harold has to find ingenious ways to catch sight of his own reflection and to shave without cutting his own throat. Harold's son rollerskates in the hallway and is told by Mother to take his skates off; but when Harold comes into the dining room to eat breakfast, a skate is now waiting in the doorway for him to slip on. Halfway through proclaiming what a beautiful morning it is, he slips and tumbles, head over

heels over the threshold and into the dining room. The voice is interrupted, so to speak, by the body; and the two are set at variance again
over the breakfast table. If Uncle Bean dies, asks Junior, do we get to
go to California? "Ur, no," says Harold, to appease his wife, nodding
the affirmative to his son. "See, we gets to go," announces Junior to his
sister, "When Pop said 'No' he shook his head 'Yes.'" Harold shuffles
in his seat, and we hear a thud where an attempted kick strikes the chair
leg instead of his darling son's shinbone. "What's the matter, Pop?"
taunts Junior. "Don't you love me any more?" "Certainly I love ya,"
rasps Harold, raising an arm to wallop the little brat.

The integration of physical and verbal humor in these moments
forms a comedy of contradiction and containment. Harold's feelings
of captivity, both in the domestic sphere and at work in his grocer's
store, are vividly rendered through the way his body is seemingly
ambushed and ensnared by dormant physical objects: rollerskates,
feathers, telephone wires, a barrel of molasses and a porch-front bench.
In a brief moment of respite from serving customers, Harold rests his
foot on a chair and gazes longingly at a photograph of a Californian
orange grove, with its bountiful trees stretching in rows to the distant
horizon. "How about my kumquats?" demands an impatiently waiting customer. "Coming, coming," calls Harold, stepping into a
wastepaper basket and jamming his foot in its wire mesh. The constraints of everyday life extend to language and speech: Harold's wife
insists that their surname, Bissonette, is pronounced Bisson-*ay*; at one
moment she instructs Harold to "wake up and go and sleep"; and
Harold's deferential way of speaking, by force of habit, is typified by
a chronic repetition of conciliatory phrases ("coming, coming," "I'm
sorry, I'm sorry"). That most characteristic expression of W.C. Fields —
the cynical rasping that emanates from the side of his mouth — is
employed here not merely to convey a sidelong, cynical attitude to the
world, but also to suggest a containment of body and voice, striving
to keep in check all the underlying tensions of bourgeois family life.

The hallmark routine of Danny Kaye, by contrast, is a frenetic
use of the voice in a manner that might be described as "verbal
slapstick."[9] Just as Buster Keaton contorts his whole body to evade or

sidestep a pressing world, Danny Kaye is an equivalent contortionist of the tongue, lips and voicebox. In an early sequence from *Up in Arms* (1944), Kaye steps out of line in a cinema lobby to enact a one-man parody of the generic film musical, playing all the parts himself through some dazzling vocal shifts: the female chorus-line, setting the mood; our hero, the singing cowboy; the girl, an opera soprano who really wants to be a tap dancer; her stuck-up English father who is really a German spy; and the Bolivian bombshell who rounds off the "movie" with a conga line finale. He even kicks off proceedings by delivering the opening "credits," beginning in an excessively operatic vein — "Manic Depressive Pictures Presents..." — and itemizing the "authors" with a rolling tongue in a melody starting cheerfully but spiraling swiftly downwards into absurdity:

> Screenplay by Gluck. From a Stage Play by Mahtz. From a Story by Blipp. From a chapter by Ronck. From a Sentence by Dokes. From a Comma by Stokes. From an Idea by Grokes. Based on Joe Miller's Jokes.

From here he shifts gear once again, now launching into a flurry of names and roles and nonsense words that is as much a parody of movie credits as it is a spectacle of the voice pushed to its physical limits. As Kaye scans the imagined screen with darting eyes, the camera moves into close-up to detail his effortless enunciation, delivered in a corkscrew melody and at breakneck pace, almost too fast to follow:

> Art-Direction-Fink-Arbuff-Interiors-Manurf-Arpupp-Photography-Atlans-Otech-Recorded-Sound-Asneedles-Beck-Upholstery-by-Zackery-Nack-Nackary-by-Thackeray-Traxickery-by-Dickory-and-Dickory-by-Dock![10]

Kaye's tongue-twisting stresses phonetics over seman-

Danny Kaye: Master of verbal slapstick.

139

tics, pronunciation and hectic phrasing over matters of signification, and assonance and offbeat rhyming over referential meaning. In this way, his performance spectacularly foregrounds the physical process of articulation. The term "verbal slapstick" is thus fitting to describe Kaye's comedy not simply because his syllable-munching recitations approximate the pace and spirit of a slapstick chase — *we* do the chasing, so to speak, and need to keep up — but because his performance brings out the *physicality* of the voice, pleasurably reinstating the voice as a product, indeed a facet, of the body.

Jerry Lewis also presents speech as primarily a physical undertaking, but does so in a very different fashion. His screen persona, at its most screwy, tends towards an inelegant failure to communicate, a shortcoming that mirrors the way his attempts to carry out what should be rather straightforward physical tasks tend to become prolonged exercises in abject malfunction; body and voice are thus ironically unified through a failure to control either. Hinting at this curious synthesis, Raymond Durgnat elegantly conflates body and voice when he describes how Lewis "stutters with his feet [and] trips over his tongue";[11] and, in a similar vein, Frank Krutnik notes how "Lewis's performance disconnects the mouth from the mind, transforming the speech act into an expressive vehicle for the unruly body."[12] Such a tendency is evident in *The Errand Boy* (1961), a film that repeatedly returns to matters of the voice. Starting work as a mail clerk and general dogsbody in a Hollywood studio, Jerry is repeatedly unable to pronounce the names of his superiors. His ludicrously offbeam efforts retain only the very broad outline of names as spoon-fed to him by increasingly frustrated colleagues, so that Babe Wosenthal becomes Ben Payfinton, Mr. Wabenlotnee becomes Mr. Habenaben, and Mr. Verdmitnen becomes Mr. Varmibben. Bewildered by too many names and roles and places, Jerry finally regresses into gibberish and wanders off, babbling to himself distractedly. Here Lewis's vocal playfulness balances the humorous presentation of a wretched idiot, pathetically unable to repeat, parrot-fashion, a short collection of names, against the sense of an oppressive factory system, too large and knotty to accommodate the individual. It is typical of Lewis's comedy that one is never quite sure whether

140

Jerry's incapacity to adequately conform is more a mark of his personal mental-physical defectiveness or of an over-demanding society.[13]

Jerry's patent inability to fit into social groupings is pictured in the following scene in terms of his body. When a rapidly forming queue of extras blocks his path, Jerry tries to squeeze through between two men in the line. Awkwardly going in left arm first, he pushes his head into the gap and presses with his face against the taller man's chest, trying to prize the two men apart. Then, using his elbows, he juts into the space, resting for a moment with his elbow dug into the smaller man's shoulder blade and his hand on his own head. Jerry's humorously ape-like gestures here exemplify the peculiarity of his body in relation to others, manifesting a distinctly primordial quality that hinders his assimilation into the social world. Moreover, as Jerry wriggles through and bursts out the other side of the line, the impression gained is of an *abject* body, expelled from the larger body of conditioned, orderly citizens. The scene is organized so that the queue forms across the screen horizontally, between Jerry and the camera, so that the angle of view accentuates the contrast between a rigid, tightly-grouped and systematic line of bodies and a single, writhing figure at the center of the frame. Shot in this way, the queue evokes a misfit squirming amidst

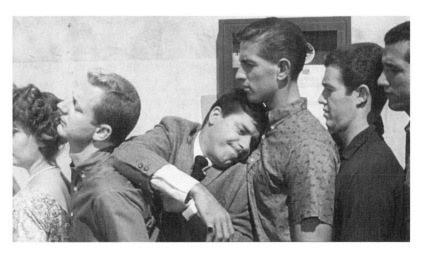

The abject body of Jerry Lewis. *The Errand Boy* (1961).

a military line-up; and indeed Lewis's films repeatedly return to the motif of the regimented body—the line-up of hotel porters in *The Bellboy* (1960); the bodybuilder in *The Nutty Professor* (1963); the marching businessmen in *Who's Minding the Store?* (1963)—setting off the contrast with Jerry's uncoordinated, faltering figure.

"Get back in line, will ya?" scolds an overworked studio-hand as soon as Jerry makes it through the other side. "And no talking!" he snaps, before Jerry gets a chance to reply. "Things are tough enough without suggestions and constant interruptions!" Upon which Jerry is shoved back into the queue he didn't want to join anyway, and ushered away by the procession of conformists, twisting his neck back to vigorously shake his head at the studio-hand, tongue hanging out the side of his mouth. Both body and voice are compelled by an overarching authority in Lewis's films, continually exposed to disapproving eyes and ears. Jerry is frequently told to keep quiet, even when he hasn't even opened his mouth. In *The Bellboy*, these chastisements for speaking become a running joke, since Jerry doesn't utter a word for the duration of the film (save for a single line at the film's close). "We don't talk back!" cautions his supervisor; "I don't care what you want to say...," says a condescending hotel guest; "Sit down, eat your food, and SHUT UP!" yells a mobster as Jerry tries to eat his lunch in peace. The recurring joke implies Jerry's wordlessness to be a symptom of his subordination. Moving endlessly between different tasks as accentuated by the film's episodic structure, Jerry's drifting, contingent existence in the hotel, never rooted in his own words, is shaped only by a perpetual following of orders.

In *The Errand Boy*, Jerry's voice, a garbled stream of mangled words, is persistently out of place. Finding himself on a film set as part of the chorus in a musical, Jerry is first dumbfounded as the other extras begin to sing a refrain, and then over-enthusiastic—raising his squeaky voice to wail "Wacka-do wacka-do wacka-do-do-do," out of tune, out of synch and hopelessly out of line. His inadvertent disruption of proceedings by means of the voice is mirrored in a later sequence when Jerry ruins a movie premiere, having managed, inexplicably, to sound-dub his bleating voice over that of the leading lady. This substitution of the respectable by means of the inappropriate is characteristic of Lewis's tendency to dissolve order into disorder through a single rogue element (typically Lewis's body, or his voice). The gag is also characteristic of Lewis's comedy in that it foregrounds the illusion of unity in the cinema — in this case, the unity of body and voice that synchronized sound tries to affirm.

This characteristic is an attribute of what is perhaps the most accomplished sequence in *The Errand Boy*: the scene in which Jerry finds an empty boardroom and acts out being the boss. Booming, authoritative voices have to this point firmly distinguished those in positions of power within the studio hierarchy, such as Jerry's boss in the mailroom and the head of the studio. By contrast, Jerry's subordinate status has been marked by a malfunctioning, squeaky voice, always subject to efforts to control it from higher up the food chain. In this scene, one of those surreal flights of fancy that pepper Lewis's films, Jerry draws upon a non-diegetic big band musical number to provide him with the necessary voice of authority. Taking a load off in the boss's leather armchair, he assumes the role by helping himself to a fat cigar and lighting it in his mouth. On the soundtrack, a plucked double bass

Jerry Lewis plays the swaggering big man with a voice of a brass ensemble in *The Errand Boy* (1963).

tentatively begins a steady rhythm. Then, as he pulls out the cigar and gestures towards an imaginary board-member across the table, the first musical phrase, a brassy double-stab, issues from the soundtrack to fill his rubber-mouthing of a word of instruction to his associate. Pointing around the table to the rest of his invisible board members, he now enunciates more directives, mouthing seamlessly to fit the shape and rhythm of the song. The brass ensemble provides a sound that perfectly embodies the rasping voice of an egotist. His gestures are of the swaggering big man, almost cross-eyed in his arrogance, proclaiming his superior status with sweeping hand movements and an outsized puff on his cigar in the brief interval between melodic phrases. As the music builds up to fever pitch, he spins full circle on his leather chair and launches into an angry tirade, banging on the desk and waving his arms as the trumpets blare furiously to the motions of his mouth. Body and voice are paradoxically at one with one another here while at the same time being fundamentally split. The realization of synchronicity is so flawless that the music really seems to emanate from his throat, consolidating the caricature of boardroom management so wonderfully conveyed by Lewis's gestures. Yet the achievement of voice is shown to be little more than an illusion of authority: the yoking of commanding sounds to an absurdly gesticulating body.

7

Body and Gender: Female Performance in Hollywood Slapstick

In *Ella Cinders* (1926), Colleen Moore plays a small-town girl who slaves as a domestic servant for her step-family and aspires to become a Hollywood actress. Her big chance arises when a film company launches a beauty contest in her local town, and so Ella heads to a photographer's studio to have her portrait taken. In front of the lens, she prepares herself by assuming a series of clichéd poses of conventional femininity: the demure young innocent with a finger to the lips; the wide-eyed starlet, beaming skywards with hands behind her head; the glamorous rose, with fingers to her neck and a veil softening her face, gazing longingly into the distance. The comic twinkle with which Moore performs Ella's posturing ensures that each pose is seen as an absurd affectation; the excessive commitment with which she launches into each role stresses the ingenuousness of Ella's strivings but the hollow artificiality of the roles themselves. Then, as the photographer prepares to take the picture, a fly lands on Ella's nose and she crosses her eyes, wiggles her nose and puffs upwards with her mouth to dislodge it — just as the shutter is pressed. The resultant photograph is an image of contortion that is portrayed within the film's own terms as antithetical to the orthodox image of untroubled beauty expected of women in pictures. Yet, surprisingly enough, Ella wins first prize in the contest. "Beauty means nothin,'" explains one of the judges, "The movies

145

need newer and funnier faces." Upon which Ella sets out to Hollywood where her new career awaits — in comedy.

That the contest turns out to have been an elaborate hoax — and the studio gates are shut when Ella arrives — is self-consciously suggestive of the limited possibilities afforded to women as stars of Hollywood comedy. For all the battleaxes, man-eaters and sweethearts that populate slapstick comedy at the sidelines, very few women have performed (and even fewer have sustained) the kind of raucous physical horseplay that Keaton, Chaplin, Lewis and Laurel and Hardy frequently enact in their films. To trace the complex intertwining of industrial and ideological reasons for this under-representation in slapstick is beyond the scope of this book — indeed, could constitute a whole book in itself — but a significant factor is surely the severe range of expectations that have traditionally governed the female body in patriarchal society. Not least of these is the dominant ideal of feminine beauty (far from "meaning nothin'" as the bogus contest judge asserts) which seems fundamentally at odds with the clumsiness, contortions and spectacular activity that characterize the slapstick body. As Moore's witty posturing brings to light, such dominant ideals compel the female body to be an object, doll-like and unruffled. Contrastingly, the slapstick body, as pictured in Moore's cross-eyed attempts to blow the fly from her face, is comically dualistic: at once an object within the world (such as a fly might land upon) and a subject acting on the world (such as might strive to blow the fly

Roll up, roll up: Colleen Moore is playful with gender.

away). Merleau-Ponty discovers this duality of the body in trying to articulate a first-person experience of the body: "When I touch my right hand with my left, my right hand, as an object, has the strange feeling of being able to feel too ... I apprehend my body as a subject-object...."[1] We might say that physical comedy also discovers this crucial feature of human embodiment, through comic manifestations of the body's interaction with the world. Yet Moore's cross-eyed convolutions represent only a rare instance of this dualistic dynamic being afforded to the *female* body.

Ella's body is introduced to us as being possessed and controlled by others. In the opening sequence, Ella is shown lugging two heavy buckets of coal dust up the cellar steps in a side-on shot that accentuates the gradient of the staircase. Interrupted in her labors by her step-mother and step-sisters, each of whom summons her by yelling her name ("ELLA!"), she vacillates on the landing, grimy with soot, as to which call she should answer first. Her step-mother is most adamant in her yelling, so Ella proceeds to the old lady's bedroom first to give her a back rub with a rolling pin. To become a professional actress seems the only way out for Ella. Later in the day, she has a moment to herself to practice for the upcoming contest by rehearsing facial poses from an acting handbook. She cocks a side-glance at herself in the bedroom mirror in an unconvincing emulation of a picture marked "Flirtatious." Dissatisfied with her attempt, she moves on to the panel marked "Cross Eyes" and gives that a try instead. In a sustained frontal close-up that is as startling as it is amusing, we see Moore's eyes swinging outwards to either side; then meeting in the center of her face, the right eye squirming independently as the left eye squints and winks, the left eye darting back and forth while the right wiggles up and down. This remarkable comic feat[2] represents an extreme instance of bodily control, casting aside the passivity of more supposedly feminine poses in which eyes are meant to be immobile, glassy or sexually alluring. Reclaiming Ella's body as her own by declaring her absolute dominion of it, the moment is suggestive of the potential for comedy to unfetter the female body from the twin regimes of cultivated beauty and domestic labor.

Moore's lead role in *Ella Cinders* is a rare exception to the rule that leading slapstick performers are male. Yet even her style of performance constitutes more a comedy of the face rather than of the body as a whole. That bastion of slapstick humor familiarly known as the pratfall, for instance, is noticeably absent from Moore's performance in *Ella Cinders*, and indeed violent tumbles are rare in female performance throughout the history of Hollywood comedy. A salient exception can be found in the first third of *The Miracle of Morgan's Creek* (1944). Trudy Kockenlocker, played by Betty Hutton, is returning home woozy from an all-night party and hoping to sneak inside without her father finding out. She is still wearing her party dress and she's staggering and slurring her words a little. Her unwitting escort, Norval Jones (Eddie Bracken), asks if she can get in all right. "Can I get in all right?" squeals Trudy, heading through the garden gate. "Why, what's the matter with you, Norval?! I never had a drink in my life, and you talk as if I were swaffled or something! Good night!" At which point Trudy's trailing coat-tail snags on a fence post and she is pulled backwards, arms and handbag flailing, teetering over to one side and bumping to the ground, legs spread-eagled in the air and her dress over her head. It's a gloriously undignified tumble, all the more gratuitous for appearing to be strictly unnecessary in the development of the film's plot. What it does allow for, however, is a forceful declaration of this woman's physicality so that, when it later turns out she is pregnant with a child conceived by an anonymous soldier, we cannot possibly think of her as either a violated angel or a wanton hussy: she is simply capable of slip-ups like the rest of us. The film does not go so far, however, as to allow Hutton a pratfall as a visibly pregnant woman (or indeed at any time after we discover that Trudy is pregnant). This should hardly be surprising: a comic depiction of a heavily pregnant woman falling over would not represent an appropriate possibility, at least in this body of work. But Trudy's exemption from the field of physical horseplay is telling in that her newfound condition of vulnerability is not dissimilar from the cultural projection of this condition on to the bodies of women more generally. Viewed through a patriarchal lens, (young) women's bodies are habitually seen as too fragile, too *precious*, to slip on a banana peel or fall down a flight of stairs.

Katharine Hepburn magnificently side-steps such cultural inhibitions, denying the fragility of the female body as the madcap Susan in *Bringing Up Baby* (1938), where she trips over a stretched wire, crawls through the undergrowth, slides down a hillside and hauls a leopard up the steps of the County Jail. Her physical vitality is robustly affirmed in her very first appearance, on the fairway leading to the 18th green: towering over the ball, freely swinging her club in preparation for the shot, at once breezy and composed. The comic contrast is with the gawkiness of David (Cary Grant), lolloping over out of the shadows to claim his ball (which she is inadvertently now playing). His movements are awkward, self-conscious and shuffling; hers are assured, intuitive and fluid. Having dispensed with the ball, she spins around to face him, knowing exactly where he is without looking, and hands the club to an offscreen caddy, again without looking, letting it go with a carefree flourish of the hand. Then she strides across the fairway, the camera tracking alongside her, David hot-stepping in pursuit and the caddies in tow like the tail of a Chinese dragon. The combination of athletic energy and relaxed confidence in her stride, already drawing David away from his staid life of dinosaur bones and glass cabinets, generates the striking sense of a world of physical possibility and of a woman unself-consciously self-possessed. These qualities of assurance and self-possession are embodied by Hepburn even when her character is falling or floundering. Indeed, while her numerous accidents in the film — losing the back of her dress in a high-class restaurant; knocking out the family lawyer with a hurled rock; plunging into a river which she insists is only knee-high — all result from a certain misplaced confidence, the film is less interested in scoffing at such assurance as it is in savoring her response to the mishap: her valiant attempt at covering her underwear by walking in a two-step with Grant; the brisk way she flees from the lawyer's property with Grant in tow once again; the way she scrambles about in the water, coughing a new assertion that the river bed has changed. Far from being fazed by such setbacks, Susan reacts with spirited, if capricious, resolve. When she trips over and crashes to the floor in her apartment, she is on the telephone to David, telling him about the leopard in her apartment and forcefully asserting her helplessness: "You can't leave me alone with a leopard. No, I'm going to come and get you...." The line itself carries a contradiction between a cry for help and a promise of rescue, a tension further underlined by the way she lurches towards the camera, blending the panic of a damsel-in-distress with the charge of a knight-in-shining-armour. Her sprint is broken by the stretched wire of a table lamp, plunging her into the near-ground, and the camera pans with her movement downwards, candidly observing her physical resilience as she crashes to the floor.

On the other end of the line, hearing the crash and suddenly filled with patriarchal concern, David jumps to conclusions: "Susan! What happened? Is it the leopard?" Now in a heap on the floor but with the receiver still pressed to her ear, Susan begins to reassure him before realizing an opportunity to transform personal mishap into romantic gain. Playing the damsel-in-distress card once again, she cries out "The leopard! David! The leopard!" and smashes some dormant crockery to add to the illusion of being viciously savaged by a wild beast. Her spontaneity here, born of an earnest commitment to playfulness, is a good instance of the way Hepburn's performance is creative with gender, a creativity no doubt allowed for by the attractively androgynous qualities of her physicality, specifically her round-shouldered athleticism and sturdy elegance. Stanley Cavell argues that *Bringing Up Baby* "poses a structure in which we are permanently in doubt who the hero is, that is, whether it is the male or the female, who is the active partner, which of them is in quest, who is following whom."[3] Hepburn's combination of masculine and feminine traits is allied to the film's intricate patterns of pursuit and retrieval to exacerbate this doubt all the more. It seems no accident that at one moment in the film Hepburn dons Grant's trilby hat; nor that he ends up, in another moment, wearing a fluffy negligee. Indeed, this minor instance of mirroring forms part of a wider pattern of mirroring and matching between the sexes. In particular, physical entanglements and indignities suffered by one partner are consistently echoed in situations encountered by the other. Seconds after Susan has tripped to the floor in her apartment, David falls to the floor in his own apartment in his panicked rush to save her (so undermin-

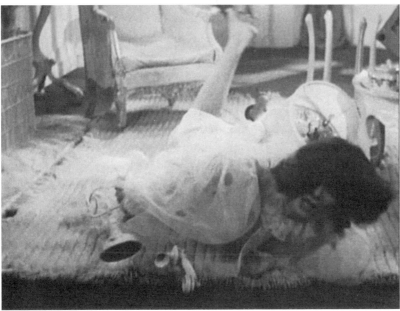

Katharine Hepburn trips and falls, as the madcap heiress Susan in *Bringing Up Baby* (1938).

Falling about with laughter: Susan (Katharine Hepburn) snags David (Cary Grant) in a butterfly net after tumbling down a bank of earth in *Bringing Up Baby* (1938).

ing any pretensions to masculine resolve). David's accidental tearing of Susan's clothes in the restaurant mirrors, as if by magic, Susan's accidental tearing of David's clothes moments before. David's inadvertent sliding down the bank when searching for the leopard in the woods is followed seconds later by Susan's accidentally sliding down after him (she is too busy laughing at him to watch her step), landing him in her brandished butterfly net and collapsing in further giggles at its appropriateness.

The mirroring of mishap declares a perfect romantic match, and is underscored by an apparent equalization of physical weight as the film proceeds, culminating in a mutual balance that is demonstrated by their catching of each other at the film's close: Susan's catching of David when he faints in the County Jail, and David's catching of Susan from the scaffold as the brontosaurus skeleton creaks and crumbles

'Swoonderful: Susan catches David when he faints at the county jail. *Bringing Up Baby* (1938).

beneath her. If Susan's airiness is stressed in her costumes in the first part of the film (her shimmering silver gown and suspended ribbons that cascade from her hair in the restaurant sequence, for instance), she seems to have invisibly acquired some solidity by the end of the film, enough to lug a wild leopard up the steps of the County Jail and to catch David's flailing body without strain. Meanwhile, David, it seems, has finally lightened up, transformed from the opening man of stone, having been successively adorned with feathers, a fluffy negligee and a butterfly net. This oblique pattern of a process of equalization underpins the film's celebration of a form of romantic compatibility based on physical congruence more than sexual difference.

Hepburn's extraordinary physical bearing demonstrates the possibility for a style of comedy based around female activity. Yet such a potential has rarely been tapped outside of *Bringing Up Baby*. Instead,

Hollywood slapstick has tended to revolve around the activity of a central male figure, with women often serving as little more than comic props. Such a situation is hinted at in a bizarre sequence from *Ella Cinders* when, having sneaked into a studio lot and fleeing from security guards, our heroine bumps into Harry Langdon, who happens to be on set. Ella pleas for his help; Harry panics and flutters around, looking for inspiration. With a guard fast approaching, Harry hits upon an idea: bending her over to form a 90 degree angle, draping her with a tablecloth, and sitting down to eat some bread and soup from the level surface of her straightened back. Moments later, having fooled the guard, Ella arises from her position and Harry gets a bowlful of steaming soup tipped over his crotch, as if the activity of women were itself a dangerous upheaval and an emasculatory threat. Indeed, in Langdon's feature films, *Long Pants* (1927) and *The Strong Man* (1926), women are repeatedly seen as threatening, sexual predators of Langdon's sheepish innocent, and in various ways the narratives of each film contrive to contain this threat in sequences that transform women into objects. In an early scene from *Long Pants*, a drug-smuggling city vamp wraps her tentacles around Harry one moment and abandons him the next. Harry is nonetheless smitten and later helps her flee jail by nailing her into a wooden box and carrying her like cargo on his back. Somehow he mixes up this box with a crate containing a giant alligator, and, as he prizes open the lid, unsuspecting of the perils within, the inference points to the comparative threat posed by the woman. In *The Strong Man*, Harry is picked up by a tall and sturdy gangster's moll who pretends to be his penpal sweetheart in order to retrieve a roll of bills that is (unbeknownst to Harry) stuffed down the back of Harry's trousers. Harry looks petrified, clutching his hat and shrinking away, as she puts her hands all over him in the back of a cab. Next, she tries to take him back to her hotel room and, finding him nervously resistant, pretends to faint outside the hotel lobby so that he might carry her up to the room. An extended sequence ensues in which little Harry struggles to convey her long, limp body up a large marble staircase, striving at first to carry her forward in his arms, honeymoon-style, but finally resorting to lugging her carcass backwards, one step at a time. The sexually

Harry Langdon hauls Gertrude Astor up the stairs in *The Strong Man* (1926).

active female has been reduced to an inert mass, yet she still represents a hazard. Too busy concentrating on hauling her upstairs, Harry carries on going when he reaches the top, backwards up a stepladder that is set out on the landing, and finally up and over the top, thumping to the floor in a heap the other side.

The comedy of Buster Keaton, most centrally based around the energetic physical activity of a central male figure, goes even further in its treatment of women as objects. As a caveman in *Three Ages* (1923), having finally won the Girl from his neanderthal rivals, Buster abruptly grabs her by her hair and drags her away backwards through the dust. Despite the undisguised brutality of her treatment, the Girl's being dragged is portrayed as a willing submission: in traveling close up as she is towed away, we see her smile broadly, fold her arms across her chest, and roll and close her eyes as if in ecstasy. Moments earlier, in order to win the Girl in the first place, Buster has climbed aboard a

catapult and been hurled across the sky, like a cannonball: another willing submission to forces greater than one's own and another example
of being turned into a human object. *Both* moments suggest the
undignified necessity of occasionally being reduced to an object, of
making oneself passive in the pursuit of happiness. Sometimes the only
thing to do is to surrender to it — and, in any case, the Girl has less
than a say in the matter.

In *Spite Marriage* (1929), Keaton builds a whole sequence around
the use of his female lead as an unwieldy object. Buster has been out
on the town with his new bride, a haughty actress who (unbeknownst
to Buster) has married him purely out of spite, to get back at a former
lover who has spurned her. She has spent the evening drowning her
sorrows with champagne, and as they get back to their honeymoon
apartment, it is clear she is a little worse for wear. She wobbles into
the room, buttressed by an attentive husband, with glazed eyes and a

Buster tries in vain to get his drunken wife (Dorothy Sebastien) to bed in
Spite Marriage (1929).

sullen expression as if she is going to be sick. Buster carefully balances her on her own pins for one moment and goes to shut the front door. Immediately her knees give way and she slumps to the floor, folding over like a rag doll. Buster secures the door, turns back into the room and promptly trips over her inert form, plunging face first to the carpet. Picking himself up and failing to resuscitate her, he endeavors to seat her on a wooden chair, trying at first to gain purchase from under her arms but finds her arms so flaccid that they slide through his grip. Instead he tries to gather her into a bundle, holding behind her head and under her knees, but her torso weighs too heavily for him to lift this way. Next he tries to pull her up to the chair rear-first, from around her middle, resting a womanly hip on the seat-edge and trying to roll her into position. But her unfolded body once again proves too cumbersome, and she sprawls to the floor once again. Buster must find a different approach. Ever resourceful, he maneuvers her into the semblance of a seated position as she lies on the floor, shifting her onto her side and bending her legs at the knees into right-angles. Then (moving the mountain to Mohammed, so to speak) he turns the chair on its side, cups the cushioned seat onto her buttocks, twists the chair and sitter onto their shared spine and hauls them into the upright position to balance. Mission achieved, it seems, for a few seconds, while Buster picks up his coat from the floor. But then gravity takes over: her head and shoulders droop once more and her bottom slides off the seat. Undeterred, Buster tries instead to put her to bed, and the process of heaving and hauling is set in motion all over again.

The entire scene is rendered in a series of long takes that emphasize the strenuousness of Buster's endeavors, accentuated by the camera's relative restraint and the woman's acute inactivity.[4] The extreme variance in terms of action and vitality is taken to mark a difference between the sexes (rather than simply between two characters who happen to be differently sexed) because it is precisely the fact that she is a woman, and he a man, that permits him to handle her in this way: in at once the most intimate and most impersonal way imaginable. His manner of touching her body illuminates his relationship to her more generally in the film, and enacts an unwitting reprisal for *her* earlier

157

treatment of *him*. His distant worshipping of this woman, cut off and raised above him by the stage and by her class, has been transformed into an ever-so-close devotion, yet the relationship remains one-sided in all the ways that matter. She remains as distant as ever, her consciousness closed off to him even on their wedding night. Her shameless exploitation of him is brought to a head here, with Buster as the suffering yet diligent young husband, ensuring her comfort even at the expense of his own. She has used him as a prop for her show of spite, an unconscious accessory to an egocentric performance. And as if to redress the balance, as if out of spite, the tables are now reversed on the level of performance: the woman becomes the unconscious accessory, the object of manipulation, the prop for Keaton's showpiece.[5]

Matters of sex and gender dominate, as the title might suggest, in the Jerry Lewis film *The Ladies' Man* (1961), in which Lewis plays the dejected and neurotic Herbert H. Heebert, jilted by his college sweetheart and terrified of women as a result. Here the female body is cast as eerie and alien, a presentation strongly reflecting the central character's attitude. This is particularly marked in the uncanny sequence when Herbert ventures into the forbidden room, rumored to be occupied by a Miss Cartilage, in the boardinghouse where he works. As he skulks around the door and into the room, the camera pulls back to reveal an all-white space: the walls, the floor, the furniture, all brilliantly, weirdly white. In the middle of the room, a black amorphous form hangs from the ceiling, and when Herbert reaches to twist the bottom nodule of the shape towards him, we see it is the head of some kind of woman-thing, its eyes and nose covered over, ashen-faced but for blood-red lipstick. "Hi, Honey," it hisses. Herbert pulls a face of revulsion, but is glued to the spot as Miss Cartilage descends upside down from the ceiling like an extraterrestrial spider. Raymond Durgnat suggests that *The Ladies' Man* is concerned with the problem of "how to be reconciled to others."[6] More specifically, it is concerned with the problem of overcoming an irrational fear of women, where projections of possessiveness and duplicity have become transfigured into nightmarish hallucinations of feminine treachery. In an early sequence, Herbert is looking for work as a housekeeper, but each front door he visits to apply for the job is opened by a voluptuous young female, eager to get some home help. The first is a sassy blonde who exclaims "Oh goodie!" and throws her arms around him; Herbert extricates himself and bolts away, bawling "Oh goodie nothing, you get your hands off me!." The second is a French sex kitten, adorned with pink bows and frills, who darts out of the front door and launches straight into a session of lovemaking, pinning Herbert against a post; Herbert hastily disentangles himself and flees once again, yelling, "What are you CRAZY LADY?!" The comic excesses here appear not so much as a justification of Herbert's fears as a projection of them onto the world around him. The artificial feel of the studio-lot locale gives the sense that what we are seeing is not reality, but an expressionistic rendering of Herbert's gynophobia. This sense is amplified by the setting of the Hollywood boardinghouse, an undisguised studio soundstage that lends a dreamlike feel to what begins to seem like a materialization of Herbert's subconscious: disjointed, surreal, cut off from the surrounding world, and occupied by phantom figures of terror and comfort and pleasure and menace.

Herbert's fear of women is explicitly shown to stem from unresolved Oedipal anxieties: he screams for his "Ma!" every time things

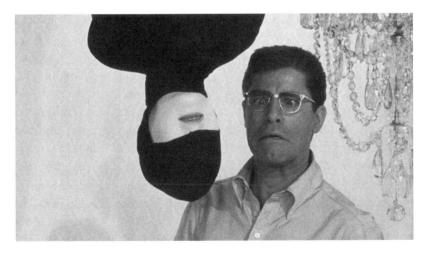

The spider-like Miss Cartilage (Gretchen Houser) descends from the ceiling to give Jerry Lewis the chills in *The Ladies' Man* (1961).

159

get frightening, for instance, and when the door to the boardinghouse is opened by a stout, middle-aged matron (Kathleen Freeman), Herbert leaps into her arms yelling "I'm safe! Oh, I'm safe! Oh, I'm so glad I'm safe!." But the boardinghouse, it turns out, is not safe. The tenants are all perky young actresses, eager to share a moment with Herbert at every opportunity, and, as if this wasn't enough, the boardinghouse pet, named Baby, can be heard roaring ferociously from behind a closed door where it devours huge carcasses of meat in a matter of seconds. If the full force of Herbert's fear of predatory women is transferred onto this unseen beast (named after a pet name for a girlfriend), and his covert desire for women to be sexless is projected onto the figure of the matron, the female tenants themselves embody an uncomfortable tension between being alluring and inexplicably threatening. This tension is at its most volatile when Herbert helps a young actress rehearse for an audition. Without warning, she oscillates between roles of the doting and vengeful lover, delivering tender lines of romance before screaming and slapping his face, caressing it the next moment, before slapping it once again. There's something eerie and unhinged about these women, even under normal circumstances. Our first sight, or vision, of these tenants getting up and going to breakfast encapsulates the film's presentation of femininity, and female bodies, as strangely menacing. While Herbert is asleep upstairs, having arrived the night before and with no clue about his new housemates, the camera swoops around various of the girls' bedrooms (which are open to view having no fourth wall), showing the occupants getting dressed and ready for the day. The style of the sequence resembles a Hollywood studio musical number, with its vivid primary color scheme, big band music, choreographed movement and myriad female bodies on display. But the tone of the sequence is complicated by the way these figures look and move, and by the sheer excess (vibrant colors, bombastic music, vast studio setting) that marks their presentation. A girl in bright red pajamas lies face up on her bed, begins clicking her fingers to the music (her roommate is playing the trombone) and then suddenly jolts upwards, puppet-like, into a sitting position. In another room, one girl is applying lipstick (we can see her "through" her dressing table

160

mirror) while another is rhythmically brushing her hair, and a third in the background is perfunctorily browsing the pages of a glossy magazine, blank and impassive, each moving mechanically to the music's rhythm like so many robotic wax dolls. The composition groups them ever so neatly, with the colors of costume and decor keeping each outline discreet and unfussed, providing an artificial, constructed feel to the shot. The camera glides laterally to the right to view the adjacent room, where more girls are occupied in feminine activities. One girl applies invisible hair spray, a second in a nightdress plays a golden harp, while a third sits on her bed sorting records, twisting them over and arranging them into a pile, the movements of her head and hands repeated over and over, the same each time, like a jukebox. Downstairs in a bright pink room, another girl briskly brushes her hair to the repeated musical phrases on the soundtrack, while her roommate performs the repetitive moves of aerobic exercise in front of a full length (but still see-through) mirror. Meanwhile the film sporadically cuts to Herbert upstairs, still asleep and lying with his bottom in the air and his head in the pillow, like an ostrich with its head in the sand. This crosscutting generates the persistent impression that Herbert is dreaming up these images of decorous, orderly, mechanical women,

Strangely menacing images of feminine normality in *The Ladies' Man* (1961).

and that his dream is at once a fantasy of uninhibited voyeurism and a nightmare of MGM proportions.

Ironically, some of the most memorable female roles in physical comedy have been performed by men. Cross-dressing has played a significant part in comedy since the beginnings of cinema (and on the vaudeville stage before it). Lewis continues this tradition in *The Ladies' Man*, as if to fuse his character's Oedipal complex with his narcissism, by dressing up in drag as Herbert's mother. Indeed, there is a playfulness with gender roles throughout this film that is exemplified by the otherworldly sequence in which Lewis dances the tango with George Raft ("You be the girl," Lewis tells him). Stan Laurel also plays the girl, charmingly, in his role as Agnes the maid in *Another Fine Mess* (1930). Stan and Ollie are hiding from the cops inside a mansion, and pretend to be master and servant when an aristocratic couple turn up at the door wishing to rent the place. Ollie squeezes into the too-small

Stan Laurel as Agnes the maid in *Another Fine Mess* (1930).

smoking jacket of Colonel Wilberforce Buckshot, and hams up his usual mix of brashness and preciousness to sufficiently convincing effect. At first, Stan takes the role of the butler, slouching in a baggy tuxedo, but pretty soon Lady Plumtree asks to see the maid. With Colonel Buckshot giving Lord Leopold Plumtree a tour of the upstairs, "Agnes" suddenly shows up on the landing, a slightly gawky young lady wearing a pinafore, clutching a dustpan and bearing remarkable resemblance to the butler ("They are twins," explains Buckshot. "One was born in Detroit, and the other in Mee-ah-mee."). Plumtree tells her that when she sees Lady Plumtree to give her his regards. Agnes curtsies and her knickers fall down around her ankles; then she turns to descend the stairs and plunges headfirst, tumbling noisily down the steps. It is difficult to imagine such undignified treatment of a woman played by a woman. What is the joke here exactly? That Stanley makes a clumsy woman? He makes a clumsy man, although the butler suffered no such violent mishap. As Agnes sits dazed at the bottom of the stairs, knickers still round ankles, and a dustpan clanks down onto his/her head, the gag resides in the roughness of the handling that is suddenly allowed for by the drag act. The supposed resilience of the male body here allows for a forceful presentation of the day-to-day indignity of a housemaid.[7]

There follows a charming scene in which Stan has a girl-to-girl chat on the couch with Lady Plumtree. Laurel's performance is proficient here in conveying Stan's enjoyment of the newfound possibilities of sisterliness. He giggles girlishly, mops his eyes with his pinafore, gives her a teasing shove (a little *too* roughly, like the way he pushes Ollie when provoked). The interclass formalities of mistress and maid are dissolved for a moment as Lady Plumtree gives Agnes a sisterly hug. And in a marvelous conflation of class-specific feminine gestures, Agnes distractedly files her nails with a featherduster: Stan has already so embraced the role that he is able to be absent-minded within it.

This is a particular kind of cross-dressing where the humor arises not from the man's resistance to being dressed as a woman (as Cary Grant resists it in *I Was a Male War Bride* [1949]), but from a kind of acceptance and even embrace of the newly-designated role. Here the

"Agnes" (Stan Laurel) files her nails with a feather duster as she and Thelma Todd share girl talk in *Another Fine Mess* (1930).

adoption of strongly gendered behavior is seen not as a restriction but as a kind of liberation. Stan's body is not so much held back by his dress and wig as freed up to perform a whole new range of actions and gestures. We see this liberation at force in what is perhaps the most famous film in the cross-dressing tradition, *Some Like It Hot* (1959), in which Tony Curtis and Jack Lemmon disguise themselves as female band musicians to escape from the mob. As soon as Joe and Jerry (now Josephine and Daphne) have boarded the train to Florida with the all-girl orchestra, Jerry (Jack Lemmon) launches himself into the part, perching himself among the ladies, wagging his head and nattering at the double: "I have the most divine seamstress, comes in just once a month, and my dear she is *so* inexpensive...."

The film is a carnival parade of stereotyped gender roles, from society girls to coin-tossing gangsters, from sour old maids to dirty old men, from debonair bachelors to dizzy blondes. Each of these is broadly

played, self-conscious and
affected to the point of
seeming parodic. As such
the film offers the most
extended exploration in
film comedy of the idea of
gender as a performance,
rather than as a biologi-
cally determined way of
simply *being*. This is most
clear in the case of Tony
Curtis's grotesque lam-
poon of Cary Grant in the
role of the suave millionaire (a film star playing a
character playing a film
star playing a character),
trying his level best to
woo Marilyn Monroe's
Sugar Kane, herself an
almost grotesque formula-
tion of the ditzy dumb
blonde. For once, Mon-

Jack Lemmon as Daphne (with Joe E. Brown
as Osgood Fielding III) in *Some Like It Hot*
(1959).

roe's overconscious manner of delivery is an asset, in a movie that seeks
to dispense with any sense of the natural. In laying emphasis on the
effort to *achieve* femininity, gender is denaturalized, revealed as nothing more than a broad set of gestures, postures, costumes and attitudes,
purposefully assumed if inadequately effected.[8]

The commonly-held notion of an *essential* link between sex and
gender — that is, of a straightforward causal relation between biology
and behavior — meanwhile wilts under the comedic spotlight. Nevertheless, the body is central to the performance. Dressed in skirts and
wigs and caked in make-up, Joe and Jerry (Curtis and Lemmon, respectively) totter on high heels along the station platform, ready to join the
all-girl orchestra aboard the southbound train to Florida. The camera

tracks with them as they move, and a pair of close ups reveals the relative success of each disguise. Joe could pass for an elegant, if slightly butch, female, his mouth pursed into feminine lips and his habitual bull-like stare softened into a cowish gaze (aided by an acute awareness of the threat of imminent death). Jerry, beside him, having turned

Top: Sometimes it's hard to be a woman: Tony Curtis and Jack Lemmon strut their stuff. *Bottom:* "It's a whole different sex!": Jerry (Jack Lemmon) isn't quite built for this role. Both photographs from *Some Like It Hot* (1959).

to look at Joe's performance of feminine poise, attempts it himself, raising his neck, cocking his head slightly and widening his eyes, trying to look composed and demure. His version of Woman is thus a copy of a copy, and he is so busy *trying* that he treads down on the side of his high-heeled shoe, twists his ankle and stumbles to a halt. "How do they walk in these things, huh? How do they keep their balance?" Jerry whines, aggravated by his failure. "Must be the way the weight is distributed," says Joe. Presently, Marilyn Monroe steps up alongside the train as if to show them how it is done, accompanied by sassy jazz music, breathless and pouting and wide-eyed, gracefully distributing her voluptuous weight from side to side as she glides on past them. Covetously, they stare at her shapely rear. A jet of steam shoots from the side of the train, and she's momentarily thrown off her stride as she twists round to see what it is, but her balance and feminine posture are swiftly, effortlessly regained. "Look how she moves!" cries Jerry. "It's just like Jell-o on springs. She must have some sort of built-in motor or something ... I'm telling you, Joe, it's a whole different sex!" Gender may be a performance, but not everybody is built to play Hamlet.

8

Body and Pain:
Brutality and Suffering
in the Slapstick Tradition

Depictions of pain and suffering are often important components of comedy that veers towards the more brutal side of the slapstick genre, and few depictions have been more brutal, or more vividly *painful*, than the early sequence in *There's Something About Mary* (1998) when Ted has an accident in the bathroom. Gawky teenager Ted (Ben Stiller, sporting a '70s mullet and bulky braces) could scarcely believe his luck when high school beauty Mary (Cameron Diaz) asked him to go to the prom with her. Now the big day is here, and Ted arrives at Mary's parents' house in a tight-fitting (and supremely naff) grey tuxedo to collect her. While Mary is upstairs making some last-minute adjustments to her dress, Ted visits the downstairs bathroom. As he urinates, he looks out of the window, where a pair of doves nestles on a nearby tree. On the soundtrack we hear the opening lines of "Close to You" by the Carpenters ("Why do birds suddenly appear. .?") and Ted gazes, misty-eyed, at this pair of heralding lovebirds, hearing the music in his mind. Suddenly, the doves take flight, and the shot of the birds representing Ted's point-of-view shifts focus to the farground, to the open window across the courtyard, where Mary's mother helps alter the dress, and Mary stands alongside wearing only her underwear. They notice Ted watching; a mobile camera from outside Ted's window swiftly

8. Body and Pain: Brutality and Suffering

Ted (Ben Stiller) has an accident in *There's Something About Mary* (1998).

closes down on him as it dawns on him what his looking must look like. Mary's outraged mother covers her daughter with a blanket and ushers her away from the window. Ted stutters some sounds of refutation, and in panic and frustration turns away from the window and yanks up his trouser zip with full force. The horrible, muffled sound of the zip makes it immediately clear what he has done. Ted stares for a second in disbelief, still bent over, before releasing an agonized scream.

The film cuts outside to the suburban street, where a mother shepherds her child away from the sound of screaming. Back in the house, Mary's family are now gathered outside the downstairs bathroom, where Ted had been hiding for over half an hour. Mary's mother whispers that she thinks he is masturbating. Mary's step-father reluctantly ventures inside the bathroom, and without much compassion enquires about the situation ("What did you do, shit yourself?"). Ted stands facing the wall. "I got it stuck." "You got what stuck...?" asks the father. "It," says Ted, and the father instantly lets out an "Ohhh!" and his hands instinctively leap to his own groin. From here on in, the situation becomes ever more farcical: the father perches on the toilet seat to have a closer look at the injury, recoiling in horror and nearly falling off the seat when he sees the damage; to the victim's mortification,

Mary's mother is then called in (being a dental hygienist she is close enough to an expert on such matters), and, after the initial shock, she performs some rudimentary anatomical analysis of what exactly it is that is stuck ("I think it's a little bit of both," winces Ted); next, like something out of a Sesame Street nightmare, a moustachioed policeman appears at the bathroom window, responding to reports of a lady (a *lady*!) screaming, and reprimands Ted for his carelessness before climbing into the house; finally, and even more unfeasibly, a fireman now saunters into the bathroom too, falls about laughing at the sight of the injury (a gruesome sight we now share, gratuitously, for the first time) and cheerfully radios his fireman friends to come see. The widening circle of onlookers forms a community built around pain, and the addition of these typically macho types only exacerbates Ted's agony. The policeman steps forward to perform the necessary operation (to "back it up," as the fireman puts it), unbuttoning his sleeves in preparation. He grabs hold of the zipper, counts to three, and just as he is about to wrench the zip down, we cut to an exterior close-up of a rushing paramedic yelling, "We got a bleeder!" With sirens blaring, crowds assembling and a host of cruel rumors gathering in their midst, Ted is wheeled on a stretcher to an ambulance, suffering yet further pain and indignity as the stretcher is fumbled and dropped on its passage through the doors of the vehicle. Mary asks frantically if he is all right; Ted pulls a full-brace grimace and a feeble thumbs up, clutching his elbow from the fall, and he is bundled into the ambulance, away from Mary and happiness, forever, it seems.

The cruelty of the laughter designed to accrue around this sequence is not to be dismissed. Any sympathy we might feel for Ted's plight is spiked with a good dose of vindictive delight at his pain. Very few comedies go so far to expose the potential for malice in an audience's response to human suffering, a potential unleashed here by the ordinary circumstances out of which that suffering arises, and by the prolonged way it mushrooms absurdly with the gathering crowd and the final dash to the ambulance. It is significant to notice the way physical pain and mental anguish commingle, and become fused into an excruciating whole. The sequence is designed to induce a laughter of horror and repulsion, sanctioned in part by the broad, almost parodic, tone and manner in which the scene is played out. The inserted shot of the trapped genitals, exceeding the polite boundary of the trouser zip, seems especially gratuitous, and prompts one to ask, not only: why is it included? but also: why is it withheld as long as it is? We have already been offered a mental picture of the injury by means of such grotesque dialogue as "What's that bubble, there?" and "How the hell d'you get the Beans above the Frank?." But the visual insert, when it comes, courtesy of artful prosthetics, is perhaps more than a means of pushing the boundaries of gross-out humor. It relates to the conflict of desire around seeing that the sequence is built around in the first place. The insert appears as the point-of-view shot of the fireman, and he greets the sight with malicious laughter. The father, by contrast, is seemingly torn between an instinctive identification (grabbing his own crotch) and an excited repulsion. As viewers we share this conflicted position, caught up (as within a hastily drawn-up zipper) between identifying with the plight of Ted, on the one hand, and with the stance of the fireman, on the other, an outsider enjoying the sight of pain inflicted on someone else. We want to see the injury and we do not want to see; the delay allows for comic suspense to materialize around how far this film will go, but also sadistically draws out the threat, or the promise, of seeing; when we see it, we laugh, or wince, or both. This conflicted reaction is related to our conflicted identification with Ted, whose injury appears as a form of castrating retribution for his "accidental" voyeurism. And as if in rejoinder to the viewer's own accidental voyeurism (having shared Ted's point-of-view as it refocused to the upstairs window), the gratuitous insert of the mangled genitals finally punishes, and rewards, the viewer's wish to see.

The sequence pictures suburban community as deepening and prolonging pain rather than providing a reprieve from it. In contrast, for instance, to the small town community depicted at the end of *It's A Wonderful Life* (1946), every new bystander gathered around Ted serves to exacerbate his misery, taking him further away from the bliss of solitude (a bliss represented, in part parodically, by the nestling doves and The Carpenters' music). Indeed, the sequence is neatly organized

171

As Ted (Ben Stiller) writhes, Mary's father (Keith David) grabs his own crotch, torn between instinctive identification and excited repulsion. *There's Something About Mary* (1998).

around the progressive move from private to public realms: it begins with a single figure in a private situation and ends with the shame of being paraded before a crowd; private bodily parts and deeds are brought out into public spaces; windows and doors are transformed from safe boundaries into dangerous channels of unwanted contact, uninvited attention and further physical threat. Ted's body is presented very much as his private domain, cruelly brought out into public view and ownership only through an unlucky series of accidents.

The comedy of abject humiliation was developed most prominently by Jerry Lewis in the 1960s, notably in *The Patsy* (1964), where, in painfully protracted scenes using shot/reverse-shot structures, Jerry all but wilts under the disapproving gaze of his superiors. Yet the nightmarish/comic scenario of inadvertent exposure finds a precedent as far back as *The Cameraman* (1928), where Buster Keaton finds himself suddenly without trunks in a public swimming pool. However, while Buster suffers the discomfiture, he avoids the humiliation, and the comic pleasure of the sequence (as with much of Keaton's comedy) resides in the manner by which he achieves this avoidance unscathed. The historical shift in comic emphasis becomes more clear when one considers how we rarely, if ever, see Keaton — or Chaplin, for that matter — squirming in the agony of humiliation or writhing in tangible physical pain.[1] But in physical comedy of the 1990s, bodies are seemingly beyond the safety net.

The tradition of comic brutality is perhaps most famously embodied, if not most fondly remembered, in the films of the Three Stooges. Their slapstick routines may achieve little in terms of shape, nuance or suggestion, but their relentless presentation of comic violence does achieve the force of a sustained assault. Eye-pokes, face-slaps and nose-crunches constitute primary units of communication between the Stooges, and pretty much anything else goes. In *Disorder in the Court* (1936), Moe performs a practical demonstration of a witnessed attack by grabbing Curly by the neck, clouting him on the cranium with a mallet, pushing his head inside a metal vice and twisting as far as it goes. In *Brideless Groom* (1936), Larry pulls the jaws of an animal trap from off Moe's rear, only to be rewarded with a violent slap in the face. In *Sing a Song of Sixpants* (1947), Moe grabs Shemp's nose with a pair of scissors, and later squeezes a hoodlum's head in a steaming trouser-press while Larry applies a sizzling iron to his vulnerable backside. In each instance, the victim resurfaces unscathed, countering the intensity of the violence in a declaration of the body's rubbery robustness. Cartoon-style sound effects and the use of fast-motion similarly work to de-emphasize the real-world physicality of the bodies onscreen, permitting the fantasy that painful action can be separated from injurious effects. Pain thereby becomes primarily associated with a set of mannerisms — cross-eyed gurning and emphatic twitching — that works to underline the notion that the pain of others is qualitatively different to one's own, perhaps even performed rather than truly felt at all. If this resembles a paradigm of that branch of philosophical skepticism formally known as "the problem of other minds," we might say that slapstick violence routinely invokes such a concept. How do I know that the pain of another is genuine, or that it is anything like what I experience when I experience pain? How do I know that the body of another is not entirely unlike my own — say, rubbery and numb rather than fleshy and sensitive? The seed of doubt raised by such questions (which might as well be called "the problem of other bodies" as "the problem of other minds") is a matter repeatedly circled around and played upon in physical comedy. When Stan Laurel's toe appears through the sole of his boot in *Way Out West* (1937), we wince with him as he treads down heavily and crumples it underfoot. Yet when Ollie gives the toe a spiteful tug, it stretches as if made of rubber and snaps back like an elastic band. Bodies onscreen are at once real and unreal, close to our own and yet distant from them. The comic presentation of physical pain can work to close that gap by allowing us to share, in some measure, a character's discomfort; or it can widen that gap by presenting pain as something singular, alien or fake.

Pain, and the anticipation of pain, is a major theme in the comic antics of the *Jackass* ensemble, a troupe of young white American men who perform puerile pranks and hazardous stunts for the camera and, it seems, for their own merry amusement.[2] For the *Jackass* performers, however, unlike the dominant, professional sort of stuntsmanship, pain

Stan Laurel and Oliver Hardy in a publicity still for *Way Out West* (1937).

is not an outcome to be skillfully avoided but instead is willingly antic-
ipated, even actively sought. Racing around an 18-hole course in golf
buggies in *Jackass: The Movie* (2002), the point is not to drive in such
a way as to narrowly circumvent crashing the carts, but instead to roll
them over, smash them up, in as spectacular a way as possible (and if
possible to hurt oneself in the process). This apparently inane pursuit
achieves a degree of profundity, however, in the way the group avoids
a conventional machismo and instead realizes a kind of joy of reckless-
ness, a sense of liberation from the usual stuffy world of business meet-
ings on the fairway. In contrast to that professionalized world (a world
that in its safety fails to escape the *fear* of pain), *Jackass* celebrates a
type of heroic amateurism, as when Johnny Knoxville tries to skate
down a ludicrously long handrail, knowing full well that as an average
skater he will injure himself in the process. The sequence is built around
the group's excited anticipation of his inevitable failure, and it draws
upon that great tradition of urban skateboarding where camaraderie is
forged around the valiant effort. *Jackass* serves as a testament to the
resilience of the body, its genuine capacity to bounce back, as a nose-
thumbing challenge to the cotton-wool culture of department stores,
risk management, safety regulations and healthy eating.

Despite its significant break from the tradition of physical comedy in its documentary form of filmmaking (in contrast to the more
customary form of the fiction narrative), *Jackass* nonetheless shares
important features with slapstick antecedents such as the Three Stooges,
Buster Keaton and the Keystone films of Mack Sennett. As with the
comedy of the Three Stooges, *Jackass* presents an extreme form of comic
violence and the exchange of pain as a mode of life. But unlike the
Three Stooges, *Jackass* employs aspects of style such as extreme close
ups, "unmodified" images and soundtrack and the use of highly mobile
camerawork in order to testify to the reality of the injuries on display,
and to guarantee the veracity of the stunts. This aspect brings *Jackass*
closer to Keaton's comedy, where Keaton's breathtaking stunts are
depicted in unbroken far shots that maintain the integrity of the action
unfolding before the lens, and so create the spectacle of an actually-
performed feat.[3] The ensemble horseplay, on the other hand, bears

Amateur skateboarder Johnny Knoxville hits the ground hard in *Jackass: The Movie* (2002).

more resemblance to the group antics of the Keystone Kops, not only in its anti-authoritarian streak, but also in its style of activity involving flailing bodies, careering vehicles, city locations and a whole lot of mud. In the opening credit sequence of *Jackass: The Movie*, the whole gang is crammed into a freewheeling giant shopping trolley and hurtled down a city street in a way that recalls the Keystone Kops spilling over the edges of a speeding police van, say in *The Grocery Clerk* (1920). Memorably, the Kops always acted as a single body made up of a number of identically dressed figures, and were rarely individuated — as in *A Muddy Romance* (1913), when a number of Kops who cling onto a rope being pulled through the muddy basin of a drained lake become even more indistinguishable with the accumulated filth. *Jackass*, by contrast, does individuate the various members of the ensemble — for instance, in the shopping trolley opening, with a written credit over the frozen image of each participant. But at the climax of this sequence, when the trolley finally slams into a barrier at the bottom of the hill,

Opposite, top: The Keystone Kops (circa 1914) crammed aboard a police cart.... *Middle and bottom:* The Jackass ensemble crammed aboard a shopping cart and then hurled *en masse* into a fruit stall. *Jackass: The Movie* (2002).

tipping up and hurling its load into a waiting fruit stall, the group is now bound into a single shared body, flying through the air as one and crashing into the folds of the stall.

This tension between individuated bodies and a single group body is carried over into a later sequence in the film that deals explicitly with pain. The guys have managed to get hold of a Muscle Stimulator that sends electrical shocks into little pads that can be placed over different muscles in the body. Each member takes it in turn to have the electric current applied to a part of his anatomy while the others sit around and laugh at his involuntary reactions. The choice of body parts becomes increasingly bold: starting with the cheek muscles that make Johnny Knoxville's face contort; then to the fingers of Ehren McGhehey, who wriggles about in amused discomfort; then to the chest of Dave England, whose pectoral muscles clench up and his face is convulsed somewhere between agony and mirth. Ehren steps forward to "do the Gooch" ("the spot between your balls and butthole," as Knoxville helpfully explains) and wiggles and twists to the pulse of the electric current, his trousers round his ankles and his legs waving in the air. Finally Chris Pontius, ready for the challenge, volunteers his "nuts." "Yeah, let's get it over with," replies Knoxville, instinctively, and with the pads applied Pontius dances around and screams, laughing through the pain as the rest of them howl along. It's a vulgar sequence, of course, but one that demonstrates the curious inclination towards a shared body, through the way involuntary spasms and infectious laughter are fused into a communal whole. Pain is habitually thought to be a private experience, individuating the suffering body from those who cannot know how it feels. *Jackass* challenges this idea by pointing to the sharedness of pain and to the universality of certain reflex actions. "You can't teach that," says Knoxville proudly to the camera, in a rare moment of reflection, watching an instant replay of himself curling into a fetal position having being willingly shot in the gut by a rubber

Opposite: Pain by proxy: Jerry Lewis gags, then moves on to a flamboyant depiction of self-restraint released into a dance of dementia. Alice Pearce is his charge. *The Disorderly Orderly* (1965).

bullet. In a culture that vigorously promotes the cultivation of the body by means of diet, pills and exercise, the convulsions of reflex and instinct seem to return the body to its curious organic roots.

The fact that the mere apprehension of bodies in pain can command a direct, immediate and forceful physiological response is a comic phenomenon exploited and mirrored by the performance of Jerry Lewis in *The Disorderly Orderly* (1965). Jerry is a hospital orderly who suffers from an unfortunate condition that is diagnosed in the film as Neurotic Identification Empathy, wherein he is overly sensitive to the pain of others to the extent that he feels like he suffers from the same symptoms.[4] This extreme form of sympathy pains becomes particularly acute when he has to take care of Mrs. Fuzzybee, an irritating inpatient who likes to boast to other patients about the various maladies she has been suffering. Jerry is pushing her in a wheelchair around the hospital gardens. "Morning, Mrs. Fuzzybee. How d'you feel today?" asks another resident, and Jerry brings the wheelchair to rest. "Well, just fine," answers Mrs. Fuzzybee, in her nasal tones. "Except for the bile in my gall bladder. You see, my gall bladder is perforated; it's full of these itsy-bitsy weeny holes, which means that the bile keeps coming through my gall bladder, dripping through my gall bladder through these itsy-bitsy teeny-weeny holes...." Meanwhile, standing behind her, Jerry tenses his face and narrows his eyes, half as if involuntarily picturing the hideous affliction, half as if responding to some inner shift, deep inside his body. He screws up his nose a little, like a rabbit, and as Mrs. Fuzzybee uses the word "dripping," his forehead begins to wrinkle and his eyes cross in the middle. His hand goes to his chest and stomach and searches around for movement. "It's a sieve!" she declares. "All day and all night, it just keeps dripping, dripping, dripping, dripping into my stomach, where it mixes with the acid which, Dr. Smathers tells me, is generating constantly in my poor sick intestines...." Jerry begins to retch but holds back from vomiting, swallowing with a wide mouth as if trying to get rid of some appalling taste in his mouth. He grins insanely and shivers from his torso to the tip of his head. He puts his fist in his mouth to keep from gagging, and wheezes with a tightened grimace. His facial contortions and squirming gestures are not so much symptoms of pain as attempts to control and contain his physiological reactions, to keep his pain in check and his response socially acceptable. Such an impression is heightened by his constrained position behind the wheelchair, in public view for the patients in the garden and unable to turn away, buttoned up in a white hospital uniform that begins to recall an asylum straitjacket.

"Push on, orderly!" shrieks Mrs. Fuzzybee, and struggling with internal pain, Jerry labors to push her over to another patient in the garden, to whom she now cheerfully relates the tale of her once-broken leg. "My shinbone was broken, and it was sticking out through my flesh! They had to take eighty-nine stitches in my right leg, and then the marrow in my bone dried up...." Behind her, Jerry bites his lip, feebly groans, twitches, chokes and splutters, as if his whole body were drying up like the marrow in Mrs. Fuzzybee's leg. A closer view of Jerry's head and shoulders isolates him in the frame, but the piercing voice carries on, almost as if it were coming from inside Jerry's head, torturing him from within. His legs almost give way beneath him, and he uses the wheelchair to support his overwrought body. When she has finished bragging, Jerry hobbles on, murmuring in pain as he rolls Mrs. Fuzzybee across the lawn to greet her next captive audience. "I actually have the weakest kidneys of anybody in the hospital," she crows, and Jerry's face clenches and shrivels in anguish. "Dr. Smathers told me himself, he said, 'Mrs. Fuzzybee, you have the weakest kidneys I have ever seen, of all the years I've been in this business I've never seen weaker kidneys.' Now the X-rays of my kidneys show...." As she bleats on, Jerry's body slackens for a second and he lets go of the wheelchair. Without the support of the chair, his body is released into a sort of dance of dementia, striking oddly balletic poses of agony as he lurches and lolls about in the background. With hands clasped against his upper chest, his whole body stiffens as if trying to stem the pain. His hands reach round to his lower back to clutch at his kidneys, and he shuffles with bent knees around in a circle with his elbows pointing outwards like chicken's wings. He flaps about with his hands, crosses them over his head, uncouples them as he bends over as in a stage bow. Emitting mad grunts and groans in the direction of Mrs. Fuzzybee, who blithely carries on with her story, he totters as if his feet were tied together (a hint of the ballet dancer once again) before finally staggering out of the frame. Waving his arms like a lunatic on his way back to the hospital, Jerry stops for a moment at the garden fountain to be soothed by the therapeutic sound of water, looming large on the soundtrack, dripping, dripping, dripping, like bile through a perforated gall bladder. He grins insanely, in bliss and in anguish, wails like an animal and lollops away out of sight.

In keeping with the apparent oxymoron of the film's title, the movements of Lewis's body, at once balletic and ungainly, orderly and disorderly, achieve something of a paradox: a flamboyant depiction of self-restraint. Jerry's striving to contain and mask his physiological responses, to keep them decent, is set at odds with Mrs. Fuzzybee's flaunting of her physical symptoms, past and present. Her recounting of grotesque afflictions to garden neighbors ironically remains within socially acceptable bounds; it is a badge of honor for her that she is able to relate such horrors in a relatively dispassionate way. Yet the outward manifestations of pain itself must be kept behind closed doors, away from common view (a social requirement for which the modern hospital is expressly designed), or else disguised, as when Jerry's groans of pain are heard by Mrs. Fuzzybee and he pretends to be blithely singing. Lewis's physical performance captures this contradiction between public bravado and hidden pain in the way certain of his movements evoke both the gestural repertoire of ballet (accentuated by the frontal perspective) and the tormented gesticulations of the mentally ill. In bringing the inside outside, Lewis's performance constitutes a remarkably expressionistic rendering of pain. Moreover, since Jerry's pain is psychosomatic, Lewis's performance can imaginatively convey the *feeling* of pain without the mimetic representation of actual physical injury. His gestures envision what it might feel like for the marrow in one's bones to dry up, or to have exceptionally weak kidneys. And just as Jerry's behavior is understood to mirror the imagined suffering of Mrs. Fuzzybee, the receptive viewer caught up in Jerry's suffering is at once close enough to share his pain and distant enough to laugh at it.

9

Body and Self: Embodiment and Slapstick Metamorphosis

In the 1927 short film *Mighty Like a Moose*, Charley Chase vividly illustrates the way cosmetic surgery might induce a split in the self by fracturing the body's continuity, just as before-and-after makeover photographs are designed to point up a chasm between the "old me" and the new. Finding his oversized teeth are making life troublesome, Charley heads to the surgeon to acquire a more shapely pair of gnashers, and intends to surprise his wife that evening with his new look. Meanwhile, however, Charley's large-nosed wife, Mrs. Moose, is also secretly undergoing surgery down the corridor, having her gargantuan conk adjusted to look more pleasing. When the pair emerge from surgery and meet at the elevator, neither one recognizes the other; in fact, they hit it off rather well as strangers. When they stop at a shoeshine stall, Charley eyes up this lovely young lady's ankles (perhaps he couldn't see past the nose before) and, exploiting his new appearance, contrives to get her to share a taxi ride with him. She clearly enjoys the novelty of having a handsome man make a fuss of her, and by the time they agree to meet later at a party, it is clear that both Charley and his wife have it in mind to embark on an extra-marital fling — with each other. Surprisingly, it doesn't require a huge leap of faith to believe that husband and wife would fail to identify one another. Before the operation, the buck-toothed Charley was all hunched shoulders and

183

Mr. Moose *before* and *after* dental surgery. Charley Chase in *Mighty Like a Moose* (1924).

furrowed brows, hesitant, ineffectual and squinting beneath glasses. After the operation, his whole demeanor has changed: his face is more open, his posture more upright, his gestures suave and sure. (Inexplicably, he now has no need for glasses, and he now sports a fashionable woolen golf cap where formerly he wore an older man's trilby.) It's difficult to imagine that one's entire personality might radiate outwards from one's teeth, but here we have compelling support for that possibility.

The finale of *Mighty Like a Moose* is a staged encounter between the new Charley and the old. Having finally realized that his would-be mistress is in fact his altered wife, and having decided that he can't trust her since she has been stepping out, Charley resolves to teach her a lesson. The bourgeois hypocrisy of this lesson is underlined by the way Charley continues to be duplicitous so as to demonstrate his wife's deceit. Armed with a pair of false teeth to assist the transformation to and from his former self, Charley is literally two-faced as he stages a melodramatic duel between the dashing lover and the jealous husband. Minus false teeth and wearing a tuxedo, Charley climbs through Mrs. Moose's window and entreats her to elope with him. "Fly with me!" he implores, and glides around after her in a bird-like parody of romantic chivalry. Before she has time to reply, Mrs. Moose thinks she hears her husband approaching, and hides her lover behind the curtain to the adjoining dressing room. Luckily, the dressing room has a back door leading to the upstairs landing, so that Charley is able to sneak out into the corridor, don a dressing gown over his suit, put in his false teeth and remove the bowler hat, before bursting through the bedroom's front door, holding an accusatory pose at the door in his role as jealous husband. He feigns a shiver as he looks at a press photograph of the illicit couple in a newspaper, checking the image against his newly modified wife, and threatens her with divorce before storming out. Now Charley the lover reappears from behind the curtain in full Don Juan mode, advancing towards his beloved with arms encircling her and his chin held high like Valentino. While she's distracted in a moment of ecstasy, he raps on the door behind her, and acts out wild alarm at the sound of Mr. Moose preparing to enter. Charley darts back behind the curtain, and, seconds later, appears again as the husband at the door, in an apparently unbroken shot that seems to authenticate the impossible swiftness of the costume change.[1] It's *almost* as if Charley can be in two places at once. His transition from lover to husband is not quite so instantaneous as to defy belief, but fast enough so as to appear to test the natural limitations of embodiment.

The entering-and-exiting of this bedroom farce culminates in a slapstick brawl between husband and lover, no matter that they possess the same body. Staged between the open curtains of the adjoining dressing room for the benefit of his wife, who sits anxiously on the bed, wringing her hands, the "fight" is inventively arranged so that, from Mrs. Moose's frontal perspective (which we often share), there appear to be *two* men slogging it out, one in a dressing gown, the other in a tuxedo and bowler hat. First, as the enraged husband, Charley launches himself off stage left in a wild attack on his rival. Following a rapid costume change in the wings, the lover is then hurled to the carpet, center-stage, clutching his jaw. Moments later, the "lover" is throttled by the hand of the "husband," whose arm appears from behind the curtain, clothed in the sleeve of the dressing gown; then, as if to restore some balance to the proceedings, the roles are reversed and the lover's

185

tuxedo-clad arm appears from behind the curtain to repeatedly punch and strangle the husband, who goofily chokes and splutters.

Back on the bed, Mrs. Moose lowers her head in distress: she can't watch any longer. Charley stops shadow-boxing for a moment when he notices her inattention. What's the point in fighting it out if the object of your squabble is not watching? He hisses to make her look up, and then resumes the attack on his offstage rival, becoming more inventive by the minute. He hangs a knee-length boot from a coat hook in the wings and swings it like a pendulum so it looks like a kicking leg, striking the floored husband repeatedly in the face; the husband grabs the boot with both hands and, getting to his feet, gets it in a headlock and bites the leather toe. By this stage the penny has dropped for Mrs. Moose (she has noticed an advertisement for plastic surgery on the front page of the newspaper, using Charley's before and after photographs as an illustration), but instead of calling a halt to proceedings, she decides to

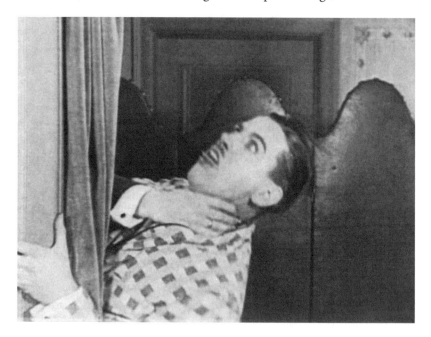

Split personality: The "lover" throttles the "husband" in *Mighty Like a Moose* (1924).

let Charley slug it out with himself, enjoying the ridiculous spectacle for what it is. The brawl has now developed into a chase, with the irate husband apparently pursuing the lover round and round a dressing screen, having switched costumes behind the screen in impossibly quick time. The chase thus appears as a series of framed images, in which the passage from left to right across the stage is briefly halted each time for a pose of heroism, trepidation or redoubled determination. In a moment of identity confusion, Charley appears in one such vignette wearing the dressing gown *and* the bowler hat. Finally, the lover is thrown to the floor from stage-right, and, knowing when he has been beaten, throws his hands up to the wife before exiting stage-left, once and for all. Charley the husband wearily emerges from the wings, crosses the threshold into the bedroom, and sits down on a chair, exhausted but triumphant. Mrs. Moose sarcastically applauds. Charley looks goofily into the camera. She shows him the newspaper advertisement and gives him a whack across the chops, so powerful that he falls to the floor. When he sits up his false teeth are no longer in his mouth. He looks around and wonders briefly if he has swallowed them, before he notices the dog, sitting in the corner, with an enormous toothy grin. Charley makes a face at the camera and the film ends.

The film thus closes not with an image of reconciliation between husband and wife, but on a note of indeterminacy about how their relationship will develop, and with yet another physical change in the form of the dog wearing false teeth. It's important to recognize how things *don't* go back to normal. We are offered an image of that normality, early in the film and before the plastic surgery, when Charley sheepishly enters his wife's bedroom, where she is sitting on the bed, and like coy lovebirds they share a brief kiss. In a profile shot of the couple that draws attention to the size of the wife's beak-like nose, Charley tries to kiss her directly, but finds her nose is coming between them and fails to reach her lips. Trying again, he cranes his head and goes in for the kiss at an angle, and this time he succeeds, although only in making contact between her lips and his massively protruding teeth. The moment is a succinct way of characterizing their relationship prior to surgery: tender if not passionate, sensitive to one another's misshapenness, but ultimately held apart by their irregular bodies. By the final reel, their relationship has drastically changed, doors are no longer entered sheepishly, and it is left wholly ambiguous as the film ends whether their married life can absorb the passion and energy of an illicit affair, or whether it will continue to be characterized by deception and distance. From this point of view, the frenetic tussling and costume shifts of the final sequence are less about Charley teaching his wife a lesson, and more about Charley struggling to come to terms with his own indeterminate status within the marriage. The brief appearance of Charley darting across the makeshift stage in dressing gown *and* bowler hat is more than a confusion of dramatic identity: it captures his desire to fuse the roles of husband and lover, to be both at once, in full view of his wife. If in the end it is the husband, buck-teeth and all, who victoriously crosses the threshold back into the bedroom, it is only because he has taken on something of the spirit of the lover, his verve and vigor and theatrical flair.

Chase's spectacular physical clowning thus externalizes a dialectical negotiation between two potential selves. We see a similar fusion, confusion and conflict between selves in Steve Martin's performance in *All of Me* (1984), where two competing souls appear to tussle for the territory of his body. It's essentially a representation of schizophrenia, although a mystical cause is ascribed to account for this weird behavior: a dying rich woman, Edwina Cutwater (Lily Tomlin), pays for a Tibetan guru to transplant her soul into the body of an attractive and healthy young lady, but the plan goes wrong and her soul ends up in the body of her lawyer, Roger Cobb (Steve Martin). Having been hit on the head by a bedpan-shaped receptacle containing Edwina's soul (it fell out of the fifth-storey window of the law offices), Roger sits on the pavement, dazed and clutching the back of his skull. A woman's voice, as if from nowhere, asks, "Where am I?," and the right side of Roger's body takes a gasp of air. "No, I can't be," the voice continues, "I just died...." Roger's bewilderment is redoubled when his right leg takes off on its own, and his right arm waves wildly around in the air: Edwina is experimenting with her new body, not merely as a place of habitation but a complex tool for movement. Roger pins himself back against a car to stop it flailing about. "What the hell is happening to

188

me?" he growls. Then a change overtakes his face, his eyes gaze into the air and his right hand places itself delicately on his upper chest. "I feel like the healthiest woman alive!" he declares in a high-pitched voice, as his right arm stretches effeminately upwards in the ecstasy of rebirth.

Split down the middle in this way, Roger's body becomes the combat zone for a battle of wills. With the left side of his body, he steps and reaches forward to pick up his sunglasses from the pavement, but his right foot remains stubbornly glued to the spot. Just as he stops trying to wrench it from the ground, Edwina decides to move the side *she* has control over, and Roger's right leg sails up into the air and plants itself down, crunching his sunglasses underfoot. Edwina wants to go back inside the law offices to find her guru, and takes some lurching steps with Roger's right leg towards the door; but Roger doesn't want to be seen by his colleagues in this state, and so tries to move in the

I feel like the healthiest woman alive! Steve Martin in *All of Me* (1984).

189

opposite direction, shuffling forward with his left leg to drag his intractable right leg behind him and stretching with his left arm and hand to grab some railings. Edwina tries to peel his fingers from the bars, using Roger's right hand to fiercely tear his left hand away. "You bitch!" Roger cries out, in pain and frustration. "How about a little respect for the deceased?" comes the haughty reply from Roger's lips, and his right hand repeatedly slaps the left side of his face in reprisal. Martin's dexterous performance divides his body to create not one but two consistent characterizations. The comic effect would be substantially lessened if the imaginary line running down the center of his body was breached by either character. Even when Edwina and Roger agree to cooperate in walking forward, Martin engineers the right half of his body to perform haughty, feminine elegance (a fluid toe-to-heel step with a sway of the hip, the right arm floating out from the elbow),

Steve Martin performs the illusion of a body split down the middle. *All of Me* (1984).

while the left half acts out a strained, masculine petulance (the left leg juddering forward in bursts, the arm pressed awkwardly against the trunk of the body and fingers scrunched into a claw).

The coherence of Martin's acting creates the vivid comic impression of *two* ghosts in the machine, fighting over the controls. It is important to notice how the visual depiction of the body as a *vehicle* is credible only in an extreme or supernatural scenario such as this one, and only through the lucidity of Martin's performance. The two-to-one ratio of souls to body allows a body/soul distinction to become visible, which under normal circumstances is difficult to present effectively. Such a difficulty is encountered when the film needs to show Edwina's soul as Roger's reflection in the mirror: how else can you visually depict Edwina's bodiless soul except by showing her body? The use of Tomlin's ghostly voiceover is equally paradoxical: the sound is unmistakably the product of a larynx, tongue and lips that are supposedly

An angel with an itch: Charlie Chaplin (with unidentified actor) in *The Kid* (1921).

lying unstirred in a corpse. The film's recourse to Edwina's body as a representation of her soul thus recalls Wittgenstein's famous dictum that "the human body is the best picture of the human soul"[2]; yet Martin's performance imagines the body quite differently, as a sort of containing vessel for the immaterial soul. The film's strange incoherence thus mirrors Roger's own internal conflict, as two apparently incompatible conceptions of the body jostle for dominion.

In a surrealistic dream sequence from his feature *The Kid* (1921), Charlie Chaplin parodies traditional Christian imagery of the immaterial soul when the Tramp transforms into an angel but remains distinctly physical in nature. Emerging from the tailor shop where we are led to believe he has purchased his wings and had them fitted (a material exchange rather than a spiritual transubstantiation), Charlie stretches his legs, and bobs his shoulders up and down a little as if to get the blood flowing to his feathered extremities. He removes his bowler hat and nuzzles his head against the top of his left wing, and uses his cane to scratch his other wing to relieve himself of an itch.[3] Similarly, when Keaton's projectionist falls asleep in *Sherlock Jr.* (1924) and his dreaming soul wakes up to separate itself from his body (in a ghostly double-exposure), the appearance of that soul is identical to Buster's body in every respect save its being ethereally transparent. He even picks up a ghostly double of his porkpie hat from a hook on the wall, and is still susceptible to tumbling head-over-heels (as we see moments later).[4] Both sequences ironically stress continuity between the character's imagined soul and his everyday lived body. For both Chaplin and Keaton, it seems, the body is so integral to the self that even an out-of-body experience is a conspicuously physical affair.

Two very different comedies, *The Mask* (1994) and *The Nutty Professor* (1963), involve a magical transformation of the body as the projection of an ideal ego. For Jim Carrey's character in *The Mask*, a radical transformation of the self involves not merely a massive shift in physical appearance, but dispensing with the laws that govern everyday physical reality. The discovery of an ancient and magical mask allows Stanley Ipkiss to transform from a mild-mannered bank clerk into what we understand to be his unconsciously-formed ideal ego, the product of too many hours watching Looney Tunes: half-man, half-cartoon figure, a tornado of energy and color. In an early scene at the bank, Stanley's flustered response to the entrance of stunning blonde bombshell Tina is a telling introduction to the character. As she sits down at his desk, he fusses with the left, then the right, then the middle drawers of his workstation, pretending to look for something, trying to look managerial. The middle drawer gets stuck and won't slide back in. Aware of Tina's gaze upon him, he dithers a little before giving the drawer a self-conscious thump with his elbow. He puts all his weight behind it to give it a shove, but the obstacle has already been dislodged and the drawer slams shut with a bang. Suddenly off balance, Stanley's upper body falls forward towards the desk, but he catches himself and immediately seeks to *mask* his clumsiness by brushing the sleeve of his jacket, officiously, straightening his back and presenting a goofy smile and a "how may I help you" posture.

The little episode captures Stanley's timidity as well as his wish to be self-confident. These characteristics are matched by his tie, patterned with colored doodles on a white background, a tentative effort at boldness against his unremarkable grey office suit. Tina notices the tie and takes it in her hands to look more closely, drawing Stanley towards her, to his embarrassment and thrill. She says it looks like an inkblot test, and says what she sees in the pattern. She asks Stanley what he sees, but, hot under the collar, he is unable to say. He reels in the tie from her fingers, waves it in the air a little, as if to say "there it is, then," and, trying to joke his way out of an intimate situation, hangs it from his mouth like a dog's tongue and makes a gagging sound (as if tongue-tied), unwittingly disclosing his feelings of animalistic lust in a gesture that is specifically enacted to put a barrier between Tina and himself. "It's a power tie," Stanley explains, refinding his voice. "It's supposed to make you feel ... *powerful*." Yet the body language that accompanies this line fully captures Stanley's feelings of inadequacy. In the pause before "powerful," he makes a limp fist with his hand and raises it up to face level, like a puny imitation of an athlete's celebration or a cartoon superhero; and on the word itself, delivered in an explanatory whisper that is almost a sigh, his hand having dropped to his side, he self-effacingly tilts his head to one side and closes his eyes, as if in acceptance of his failure to live up to the tic's promise.

Carrey's performance skillfully strings together this series of containing gestures to mark out Stanley's deep-seated inhibition. The Mask character Stanley becomes allows his body to be infinitely more assured, more active, more colorful, more openly expressive. When The Mask visits the Coco Bongo nightclub and first sees Tina performing onstage, his jaw literally drops, stretching down to the table from his rubbery green face and landing with a thump on the table, from where an enormous cartoon tongue unfurls across its surface. His eyes stretch out of their sockets on stalks, and a giant heart thumps right out of his chest and back again. He waves his legs in the air like an excited puppy, and howls with hungry approval, his skull morphing into the head of a yowling cartoon wolf. These gestures contain an amplified echo of Stanley's earlier tongue-tied gesture, and demonstrate the extent to which his feelings are ordinarily repressed. Resplendently decked out in a vivid yellow suit, capped off with a flamboyant feather in the hat, every aspect of Stanley's everyday demeanor is reversed. The Mask's magical body is able to externalize and realize Stanley's innermost desires in the outlandish manner of a Tex Avery cartoon. The computer-

Tongue-tied: Jim Carrey as Stanley Ipkiss in *The Mask* (1994).

Jaw-dropping: Jim Carrey and computer graphics as the cartoon tornado in *The Mask* (1994).

generated special effects utilize, complement and build on Carrey's renowned capacity for rubber-limbed physical comedy. Extending the elasticity of Carrey's body to a paranormal degree, The Mask bounces around corridors, sways hips to dodge bullets, changes one lurid costume after another at will, and at every turn a useful prop (an enormous mallet, say, or an entire arsenal of weapons) is magically ready-to-hand. At times this body is so stretched and warped that it ceases to represent a human body at all; the supplement of animation to the slapstick form is ambivalently realized so that the gain in vivacious spectacle is balanced against the loss of human physicality. This means, for one thing, that Stanley's wish-fulfillment is pictured as entailing a loss of the self.

In *The Nutty Professor*, Jerry Lewis similarly draws upon the Jekyll and Hyde tradition to portray a drastic transformation of the self, but reverses the usual trajectory of change, so that instead of an orderly Jekyll figure mutating into an anarchic Hyde, the monstrous and gangly body of Julius Kelp is straightened into the assured and capable body of Buddy Love.[5] Along with the physical change comes a seismic shift in personality, the extent of which is registered in the range between

195

two very different styles of costume and comic performance. As chemistry professor Julius Kelp, Lewis wears bookworm glasses perched low on the nose, a bowl-shaped haircut and a series of musty brown three-piece suits, complete with pocket watch on a chain. This caricatural appearance is intensified and nuanced by the remarkable way Lewis uses his body: the gestural habit of flicking his tongue across his buck teeth when Julius feels superior or nervous; the contraction of his throat to produce a rasping nasal voice, stuttering and twittering and chewing on sentences; the way he pushes his head forwards when he walks to suggest cerebral contemplation and the wish to hide behind his brain; the fussing of the hands in front of his ribcage, elbows squeezed inwards to conjure the deformity of shortened forearms.

As debonair crooner Buddy Love, by contrast, with his coiffured hair and snazzy suits (their clashing colors echoing the gaudy chemicals of Kelp's laboratory), Lewis fashions his body to radiate an aura

of cool arrogance: setting smooth gestures of urbanity against the stillness of his upper torso; blowing smoke around the room from his pink lips, as if laying his scent; fixing others with the surly gaze of darkened pretty-boy eyes. The humor of the performance arises from the way Lewis pushes the attributes of the lounge-lizard type towards an uncomfortable extreme of psychotic narcissism. Dealing with a challenger to his status in the Purple Pit nightclub, Buddy has barely finished pummeling

Jerry Lewis as Professor Julius Kelp in a publicity still for *The Nutty Professor* (1963).

196

Dean Martin, eat your heart out: Jerry Lewis, as narcissistic crooner Buddy Love, with Stella Stevens in *The Nutty Professor* **(1963).**

his victim before checking the fringe of his slick hair in a pocket mirror. Later on, while chatting up Miss Purdy (Stella Stevens), he smooches his own hand before generously offering it up ("Have some, baby?" he asks, as if offering up a line of cocaine). Similarly, Buddy's suave and impromptu performance of "That Old Black Magic" is pressed into the realm of parody by Lewis's hyperbolic take on the archetype of the crooner. While his body is quite constrained behind the piano, Lewis amplifies certain characteristic gestures of vocal delivery just enough to suggest the obnoxious egotism of the artist, so that little smug wiggles of the head, the conceited closing of the eyes on particular lines, and, especially, an excessive mobility of the lower jaw, strike us as grotesquely vain and self-satisfied.

The contrast between the two personalities is accentuated by the differential use of the body to flesh out two opposing types: the nerdish professor and the silver-tongued crooner. Yet, crucially, *The Nutty Professor* uses the *same* performer to play both roles. Such a decision amounts to more than just a demonstration of Lewis's dexterity and range as an actor. It points to the practice of film acting itself, illuminating that practice as a *process of embodiment*, wherein the same body, shaped by cosmetic changes and assuming a different set of expressive postures, can project utterly diverse personalities. This is a conception of the body as versatile and active in the formation of the self, rather than its passive and fixed chemical origin. Even if both Julius Kelp and Buddy Love are individually bounded by the limitations of narrow stereotype, Jerry Lewis demonstrates the capacity for radical change.

Conclusion: The Body in Hollywood Slapstick

This book has explored the presentation and deployment of the body in a range of movies in the Hollywood genre of physical comedy. Each chapter focuses on a particular relationship between the body and another element. Such an approach is itself responsive to the fact that, unlike an anatomical description in a medical textbook, the presentation of the body in the medium of film does not allow for a total abstraction of the body from its surroundings, or from other features that frame or inform such a presentation. At an elemental level, the genre's interest in the lived body, behaving in particular ways in specific locales, derives from this condition of the medium. In Chapter 2, for instance, I find an important thread of Keaton's comedy to reside in the play between athletic possibilities of the body and topographical features of the surrounding world. Keaton's visual style often reduces the body to a figure operating in a starkly composed landscape, as when, across the cleanly bisected backyard in *Neighbors*, Buster slides to-and-fro along the washing line, seeking to escape the Girl's father but ending up right in his lap. Such a tendency expresses something of Buster's distanced, even alien, perspective, from which standpoint the world is seen as a configuration of external pressurizing forces, physical and social, and the body as the primary recipient of such forces. Buster's perpetually thwarted attempts to evade these forces, especially in Keaton's chase films, can be seen to convey a wish to sidestep the world itself, to escape the conditions of being embodied. The special power of Keaton's comedy thus obtains from an acknowledgement of the impossibility of that wish, from a presentation of the body as impossible to disentangle from the surrounding world.

For these films, the fact of being embodied entails a relatively limited apprehension and grasp of the world, resulting from the narrow specificity of any single viewpoint available to an individual at any given moment. The placement of the camera in Keaton's films repeatedly invokes and magnifies such a condition, reflecting Buster's own blinkered outlook: the flattened perspective of the shot in *The Goat* in which Buster clings to what appears to be a car's spare tyre, and the framing of the sequence in *One Week* in which the train smashes through the mobile house, provide just two examples of this recurrent comic strategy. The strategy is extended and deepened in *The General*, where failing to notice, failing to recognize, failing to see what is just beyond one's line of vision becomes a principal theme of the film. Yet

Buster Keaton in a publicity still for *The Navigator* (1924).

at the same time, as discussed in Chapter 4, Keaton's hero in that film also shows remarkable focus and foresight, as when he must clear the track of obstructing sleepers and thrusts one beam forward to catapult another one free. Both tendencies derive from the condition of being firmly *in the midst of things*, a condition I have found Buster Keaton to exemplify above all other figures considered in this study.[1] The world is shown to *surround* Buster's body through far-shot framings that place him centrally in the composition, as if to reflect a subjective feeling of the world radiating out from, or closing in on, his body as its central point. At the same time, Buster's stony face articulates a sense of estrangement that ensures that he is as much detached from things as he is undoubtedly involved.

Being in the midst of things is also central to the comedy of Laurel and Hardy, where the designation of "another fine mess" is an expression of the inexorability of their being bound together again in a tight situation. Indeed, as argued in Chapter 5, the recurrence of scenes involving an awkward, too-tight proximity (around the window frame in *Busy Bodies*, under the boat in *Towed in a Hole*, in the sleeping berth in *Berth Marks*— reflects an emphasis on the *physical* dimension of togetherness. Such moments contest our commonplace notion that bodies are discrete units. In Laurel and Hardy films, depictions of the fusion (and confusion) of bodies, comically negating Ollie's mock-bourgeois sense of precious particularity (neatly captured in the fussy neatness of his gestures), offer the feeling that bodies are not entirely separate, or

Together again: Laurel and Hardy.

separable. Despite their diverse builds, the bodies of Stan and Ollie are repeatedly bound together, mistaken for one another, sharing the same space or even the same clothes. This is not the carnival body of Bakhtin's Rabelais, engaged in an interchange and interorientation with the world through the orifices of mouth and anus (see Introductory chapter), but an image of the everyday body as tied to other bodies, and as *overlapping* with them.

The idea of overlap recurs throughout this study, suggesting a pattern of comic interest across the genre in the question of where bodies end and the rest of the world begins. This is perhaps most evident in Chapter 3, where I find two of Harold Lloyd's feature-length comedies to be working around a string of gags based on the overlap between clothes and the body. More specifically, these films explore the idea of clothes as constitutive of the body, a kind of prosthetic addition that forms part of the whole, culminating in Harold's taking a shower with clothes on at the end of *The Freshman*. The deceptiveness of clothes is particularly stressed in Lloyd's comedy, deriving from the capacity of clothes to cloak and even usurp the wearer, even as they are felt to assert identity and form part of the figure we see. Indeed, in disguising or redefining the perimeters of the body, clothes can be mistaken for the body itself, as when Harold's tailor accidentally drives the needle into his client's flesh; yet this is balanced against a sense of the separateness of body and clothes, most strikingly in the way Harold's tuxedo disastrously rips and falls away in the same sequence. Further notions concerning overlap are raised in Chapter 4, which considers the extent to which the body engaged with machinery in three pertinent instances of the genre. In my analysis of a Harold Lloyd short, *Get Out and Get Under*, I discover a playful treatment of the idea of man-machine symbiosis, where technology is shown to be both enabling and constraining of the human body. While the use of gesture avoids any Bergsonian suggestion of the body-as-machine, Lloyd's engagement with the automobile presents a developing overlap between the mechanical and the organic, with Harold's car approaching sentience and responsiveness even as his body courts mindless repetition and a mechanistic drive to succeed.

Conclusion

Indeed, throughout this study, I show in various ways how Hollywood slapstick returns to the in-between body, straddling different categories, literally embodying a tension between different modes of being. Such a tendency is overt in the figure of Harry Langdon, whose body is shown to lie somehow between adult and infantile states (as discussed in relation to costume in Chapter 3). A state of in-betweenness is similarly evident in the cross-dressed bodies of Stan Laurel and Jack Lemmon in Chapter 7, and in the battleground bodies of Charley Chase, Jerry Lewis and Steve Martin in Chapter 9. The latter of these figures embodies not just a schizophrenic clash of personalities, but also conflicting categories of class and gender, and indeed my study has stressed how the comic body is often shown to bestride social categories. In Chapter 2, I demonstrate how Buster Keaton's position *between* civilizations in *The Paleface* is articulated in the use of composition and by Buster's association with the motif of the gate. Chaplin's straddling of the roles of aristocrat and tramp is expressed by means of costume and gesture, as with the cloth finger removal from *City Lights* discussed in Chapter 3, and from this duality arise other distinctive tensions in Chaplin's presentation of the body, hovering between gentility and vulgarity, indolence and vitality. Comic tensions are heightened to an unsettling degree in the Mrs. Fuzzybee episode of *The Disorderly Orderly*, examined in Chapter 8, where the body of Jerry Lewis appears at once balletic and ungainly, orderly and disorderly, in ecstasy and in agony.

This latter sequence emphasizes the capacity for pain to seemingly traverse individual bodies through vicarious identification (a capacity that no doubt also accounts for the phenomenon of collective squirming in a cinema audience given vivid comic depictions of pain on-screen).[2] Chapter 8 finds the Jackass ensemble to be emphasizing this capacity by invoking the sharedness of pain. In so doing, the antics of Jackass convey the idea of a shared body that might equally be found in Laurel and Hardy and the Keystone Kops, defying the conventional understanding of bodies as individuated and private (a notion that is implicitly invoked in the bathroom sequence from *There's Something About Mary*). Such presentations refer to what I ventured might be called "the problem of other bodies": that is, the question of how we

203

are to know that other bodies are like our own — say, fleshy and sensitive, rather than rubbery and numb (as they appear, for instance, in
the films of the Three Stooges). I suggest in Chapter 8 that such matters are repeatedly explored in physical comedy, often through the presentation of bodies that appear both real and unreal, close to our own
and yet distant from them. The spectacular musical-style introduction
to the female tenants in *The Ladies' Man* (discussed in Chapter 7)
exhibits female bodies that resemble robotic wax dolls, echoing Herbert's fear of women and proposing a vision of other bodies as uncanny
and alien. Chaplin's lighting of a match on the tuba-player's head in
A Night at the Show (see Chapter 1) comically links a skeptical attitude
towards others to the boorish manners of an arrogant drunk.

Indeed, a number of sequences analyzed in this study have
involved the tongue-in-cheek treatment of other bodies as objects or
comic props, not least the female bodies used by Langdon and Keaton

Charlie Chaplin eyeballs the conductor (John Rand) in *A Night at the Show*
(1915).

204

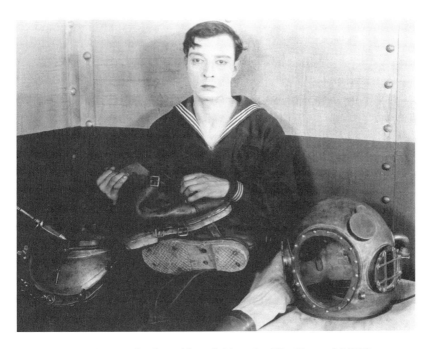

Buster Keaton in the midst of things in *The General* (1926).

as discussed in Chapter 7. Such sequences balance extremes of activity and inactivity by assigning the former to the male and the latter to the female (it has rarely been the other way round), and indeed slapstick sequences often hinge on a dualistic presentation of the (usually male) body as balancing, within a single figure, active and passive qualities. This dualism is most evident in the form of the pratfall, as when Chaplin's vigorous assault on the violin in *The Vagabond* (discussed in Chapter 1) compels a series of jitters and a subsequent tumble backwards into a large tub of water; it is difficult to see at what point deliberate action becomes involuntary reflex because one extreme seems to usher in the other. The prevalence in slapstick comedy of matters of activity and passivity, of control of the body and the loss of that control, may derive from a fundamental incongruence of human existence that is proposed by Peter Berger, following the anthropological observations of Helmuth Plessner:

The Body in Hollywood Slapstick

Man is incongruent within himself. Human existence is an on-going balancing act between *being* a body and *having* a body ... it is also possible that the sense of humor repeatedly *perceives* the in-built incongruence of being human.[3]

We might perceive such an incongruence in Keaton's repeated attempts to escape, which involve a dynamic deployment of the body (the body that he *has*), yet are often thwarted because of the momentum, weight or physical placement of his body (the body that he *is*). Such a pattern can be found in any number of gags ranging from Buster's leap onto the washing line in *Neighbors*, inadvertently returning him to the girl's father, to his swift and ingenious disguise in *The Goat* as a general on the statue of a horse, which unfortunately then starts to buckle and bend beneath his weight (both discussed in Chapter 2). All the while, the solemnity of Keaton's face, as he watches from within, humorously captures his critical detachment from the world around him and even from his own body.

This idea of critical detachment, of *having* a body, is tersely expressed by Groucho Marx in *A Day at the Races*, struggling to hold a large stack of books and using his knees to clasp a volume, muttering: "It's a good thing I brought my legs with me." This disjuncture between self ("I") and body (e.g. "my legs") is correspondingly carried by the disparity between *voice* and body, wherein the former exhibits a supple and knowing responsiveness while the latter is characterized by a stiff-backed inflexibility. As discussed in Chapter 6, Groucho's intellectual detachment from his body is contrasted with Harpo's boisterous, almost feral physicality. The self-identifying tattoo on Harpo's arm in *Duck Soup* is perhaps as succinct a declaration of *being* a body as film comedy can offer. Crucially uninhibited by a voice, this figure is also unconstrained by societal expectations, and as such Harpo offers an extreme example of the asocial body, existing in a sort of primordial state. A similar quality is conveyed by the more ape-like gestures of Jerry Lewis, registering his inability to become fully assimilated into the social world. Indeed, many of the figures discussed in this book manifest a tension between what we might call the biological and the social, hence the recurring motif of *containment* which inflects so many comic sequences, such as the College Ball scene of *The Freshman* (where Harold must conceal his body) and the Mrs. Fuzzybee episode of *The Disorderly Orderly* (where Jerry must disguise his bodily impulses). A tension between the biological and the social is particularly in attendance throughout *The Adventurer*, as when Charlie needs to mask the physical discomfort of having dropped ice cream down the front of his trousers, and indeed such a tension emerges throughout Chaplin's films in the coarse and dainty figure of the Tramp, for whom primal need and social requirement are perpetually competing demands.

Close attention to physicality is an appropriate response to a genre that places the body at its core. Such an approach requires a faithfulness to the concrete details of performance, and encourages a sensitivity to the precise way that a moment unfolds. Evoking the appearance of the body in exemplary sequences calls such moments to mind and illustrates how the significance attributed to each instance emerges from specific aspects of presentation. This is preferable to assertions of significance, and to generalized claims about films or performers, because the reader can trace the threads of the particular claim in the description of the moment itself, so that the evidence is laid out to be affirmed or contested by the reader's own sense of the sequence. A special consideration in this volume has been to remain true to the tone and tenor of slapstick — particularly in the selection of words to convey movement and gesture, and in the avoidance of a sense of preciousness or portentousness that would distort the character of physical horseplay. At the same time, such a consideration has been balanced against the desire to take the suggestions of comedy seriously, as philosophical ideas proposed in a comic register. In asking us to attend to the details of physicality, the great achievements of Hollywood slapstick offer comic meditations on what it means to have a body, to be a body, to inhabit the world here and now. The films picture human beings as wedded to their bodies, for better and for worse, and they offer this as something to laugh about.

Appendix: Films Cited

Adam's Rib (dir. George Cukor, 1949).
The Adventurer (dir. Charles Chaplin, 1918).
All of Me (dir. Carl Reiner, 1984).
Annie Hall (dir. Woody Allen, 1977).
Another Fine Mess (dir. Leo McCarey, 1930).
The Awful Truth (dir. Leo McCarey, 1937).
Behind the Screen (dir. Charles Chaplin, 1916).
The Bellboy (dir. Jerry Lewis, 1960).
Berth Marks (dir. Lewis R. Foster, 1929).
Brideless Groom (dir. Edward Bernds, 1936).
Bringing Up Baby (dir. Howard Hawks, 1938).
Busy Bodies (dir. Lloyd French, 1933).
The Cameraman (dir. Edward Sedgwick, 1928).
The Circus (dir. Charles Chaplin, 1928).
City Lights (dir. Charles Chaplin, 1931).
Cops (dir. Buster Keaton, 1922).
County Hospital (dir. James Parrott, 1932).
The Cure (dir. Charles Chaplin, 1917).
A Day at the Races (dir. Sam Wood, 1937).
Disorder in the Court (dir. Jack White, 1936).
The Disorderly Orderly (dir. Frank Tashlin, 1965).
Duck Soup (dir. Leo McCarey, 1933).
Easy Street (dir. Charles Chaplin, 1917).

Ella Cinders (dir. Alfred E. Green, 1926).
The Errand Boy (dir. Jerry Lewis, 1961).
The Fireman (dir. Charles Chaplin, 1916).
The Freshman (dir. Fred Newmeyer and Sam Taylor, 1925).
The General (dir. Buster Keaton and Clyde Bruckman, 1927).
Get Out and Get Under (dir. Fred Newmeyer, 1920).
The Goat (dir. Buster Keaton and Malcolm St. Clair, 1921).
The Gold Rush (dir. Charles Chaplin, 1925).
The Great Dictator (dir. Charles Chaplin, 1940).
The Grocery Clerk (dir. Larry Semon, 1920).
The High Sign (dir. Buster Keaton and Edward F. Cline, 1921).
His Girl Friday (dir. Howard Hawks, 1940).
The Idle Class (dir. Charles Chaplin, 1921).
The Immigrant (dir. Charles Chaplin, 1916).
It Happened One Night (dir. Frank Capra, 1934).
It's a Gift (dir. Norman Taurog, 1934).
It's a Wonderful Life (dir. Frank Capra, 1946).
I Was a Male War Bride (dir. Howard Hawks, 1949).
Jackass: The Movie (dir. Jeff Tremaine, 2002).
The Kid (dir. Charles Chaplin, 1921).
The Ladies' Man (dir. Jerry Lewis, 1961).
The Lady Eve (dir. Preston Sturges, 1941).
Long Pants (dir. Frank Capra, 1927).
The Mask (dir. Chuck Russell, 1994).
Metropolis (dir. Fritz Lang, 1926).
Mighty Like a Moose (dir. Leo McCarey, 1926)
The Miracle of Morgan's Creek (dir. Preston Sturges, 1944).
Modern Times (dir. Charles Chaplin, 1936).
Monkey Business (dir. Norman Z. McLeod, 1931).
A Muddy Romance (dir. Mack Sennett, 1913).
The Navigator (dir. Buster Keaton and Donald Crisp, 1924).
Neighbors (dir. Buster Keaton, 1921).
A Night at the Show (dir. Charles Chaplin, 1915).
The Nutty Professor (dir. Jerry Lewis, 1963).
One AM (dir. Charles Chaplin, 1916).

One Week (dir. Buster Keaton, 1920).
Our Hospitality (dir. Buster Keaton and John Blystone, 1923).
The Paleface (dir. Buster Keaton, 1922).
The Patsy (dir. Jerry Lewis, 1964).
The Pawnshop (dir. Charles Chaplin, 1916).
Payday (dir. Charles Chaplin, 1922).
The Philadelphia Story (dir. George Cukor, 1940).
The Pilgrim (dir. Charles Chaplin, 1923).
The Rink (dir. Charles Chaplin, 1916).
Safety Last (dir. Fred Newmeyer and Sam Taylor, 1923).
Sherlock Jr. (dir. Buster Keaton, 1924).
Shoulder Arms (dir. Charles Chaplin, 1918).
Sing a Song of Sixpants (dir. Jules White, 1947).
Sleeper (dir. Woody Allen, 1973).
Some Like It Hot (dir. Billy Wilder, 1959).
Sons of the Desert (dir. William A. Seiter, 1933).
Speedy (dir. Ted Wilde, 1927).
Spite Marriage (dir. Edward Sedgwick, 1929).
Steamboat Bill Jr. (dir. Charles Reisner, 1928).
The Strong Man (dir. Frank Capra, 1926).
There's Something About Mary (dir. Bobby Farrelly and Peter Farrelly, 1998).
Three Ages (dir. Buster Keaton, 1923).
Towed in a Hole (dir. George Marshall, 1932).
The Tramp (dir. Charles Chaplin, 1915).
Tramp, Tramp, Tramp (dir. Harry Edwards, 1926).
Up in Arms (dir. Elliott Nugent, 1944).
The Vagabond (dir. Charles Chaplin, 1916).
Way Out West (dir. James Horne, 1937).
Who's Minding the Store? (dir. Frank Tashlin, 1963).
You're Darn Tootin' (dir. Edgar Kennedy, 1929).

Notes

Introduction

1. It might be worth a justification, here, of my use of the term "slapstick" rather than any number of available alternatives, such as "physical comedy," "comedian comedy" or "clown comedy." Derived as it is from the sound-effects instrument used in stage comedy (possibly dating back to Commedia dell'Arte) to accompany the hitting, kicking or pratfalls being performed, what I want that word to call to mind is just the kind of broad physical horseplay that can be so unfairly dismissed as "crude," "monotonous" or "mindless" by those who fail to recognize the intricacy, variety and level of suggestion that can be and have been achieved by the best movie performers working within that comic register. By using the term, I wish to rescue the term from its pejorative uses, just as the term "melodrama" has been redeemed from kneejerk connotations of overblown "theatricality" or sentimental "excess."

2. The act of turning is a motif that runs through Chaplin's work, and not least through *The Circus.* The moment discussed here is sandwiched by the multiple twists and turns of the pursuit in the hall of mirrors, and immediately precedes an exemplary tottering-turning around a corner that leads Charlie into the Big Top arena, where the chase continues aboard a rapidly revolving platform. The movement resonates with the various U-turns engineered by Charlie as he repeatedly flees from a charging donkey, and culminates in the final turning motion of the departing circus caravan, briefly orbiting Charlie's stationary body and leaving him in an empty field, alone, with no-one to turn to. Relatedly, Andrew Klevan teases out the significance of turning in the final sequence of *City Lights* (1931) in *Film Performance: From Achievement to Appreciation* (Wallflower, 2005), pp. 21–22.

3. Most notably, when Charlie hurtles into the circus arena moments later and the appreciative audience take the continuing chase to be part of a slapstick routine. Charlie's disastrous audition for the ringmaster offers another example of this sort, as does his later ordeal on the high wire.

4. See André Bazin, *What Is Cinema?* (University of California Press, 1967, trans. Hugh Gray), esp. "The Ontology of the Photographic Image," pp. 9–16; and Stanley Cavell, *The World Viewed: Enlarged Edition* (Harvard University Press, 1979), esp. "Sights and Sounds," pp. 16–23.

5. Erwin Panofsky has written that "the primordial basis of the enjoyment of moving pictures was ... the sheer delight in the fact that things seemed to move." Erwin Panofsky,

Notes — Introduction

"Style and Medium in the Motion Pictures," in Gerald Mast and Marshall Cohen (eds.), *Film Theory and Criticism: Introductory Readings* (Oxford University Press, 1979), pp. 243–263.

6. James Agee's delineation of different types of laughter induced by silent slapstick (the "titter," the "yowl," the "bellylaugh" and the "boffo") (at the start of his article entitled "Comedy's Greatest Era" (discussed later in this Introduction), succumbs partially to this temptation by implying a straightforward connection between the production of laughter and comic achievement. Luckily, Agee's following discussion of the achievements of slapstick is so insightful that it remedies this initial impression. "Comedy's Greatest Era" in Gregg Rickman (ed.), *The Film Comedy Reader* (Limelight Editions, 2001), pp. 14–28.

7. Henri Bergson, "Laughter" in Wylie Sypher (ed.), *Comedy* (Johns Hopkins University Press, 1991, trans. Fred Rothwell), p. 92.

8. *Ibid.*, p. 78.

9. *Ibid.*, p. 74.

10. *Ibid.*, p. 79.

11. Sigmund Freud, *The Joke and Its Relation to the Unconscious* (Penguin, 2002, trans. Joyce Crick), pp. 185–6.

12. *Ibid.*, pp. 188–9.

13. *Ibid.*, p. 219.

14. *Ibid.*, p. 220.

15. Mikhail Bakhtin, *Rabelais and His World* (Indiana University Press, 1984, trans. Helene Iswolsky), p. 317.

16. As quoted in Bakhtin, *op. cit.*, p. 333.

17. *Ibid.*, pp. 320–1.

18. William Paul provides a Bakhtinian reading of *City Lights* in which he considers Chaplin's emphasis on the lower bodily stratum, but, in overstating the case, the interpretation appears somewhat forced and doesn't quite live up to the marvelous title of "Charles Chaplin and the Annals of Anality," in Andrew Horton, *Comedy/Cinema/Theory* (Berkeley: University of California Press, 1991). Frank Krutnik discusses Bakhtin in relation to Jerry Lewis, and claims that "Lewis's extremist performance ... flaunt[s] the body as a site of boundlessness and process. When severed from the cosmic function it served in medieval carnival culture, however, the grotesque body loses all connotations of social renewal, becoming instead a mode of spectacle capable of inciting extremes of laughter and discomfort, joy and disgust, identification and disavowal." Frank Krutnik, *Reinventing Jerry Lewis* (Smithsonian Institution Press, 2000), p. 11.

19. Slapstick rarely becomes gross-out in character, and, in any case, the very experience of finding bodily protrusions or excretions "gross," even of celebrating their grossness, already presupposes an implicit understanding about normal standards of taste and decency.

20. Stanley Cavell, "What Becomes of Things on Film?" in William Rothman (ed.), *Cavell on Film* (State University of New York Press, 2005), p. 9.

21. Italics in original, implying perhaps that comedy is not a philosophical treatise or argument, but more of a meditation. Alan Dale, *Comedy Is a Man in Trouble: Slapstick in American Movies* (University of Minnesota Press, 2000), p. 27.

22. Gerald Mast, *The Comic Mind: Comedy and the Movies* (University of Chicago Press, 1973), p. 23 / p. 25.

23. *Ibid.*, p. 25.

24. *Ibid.*, p. 23.

25. Frank Krutnik, *Reinventing Jerry Lewis* (Smithsonian Institution Press, 2000), p. 134 / p. 8.

26. *Ibid.*, p. 8; italics mine.

27. Steven Shaviro, *The Cinematic Body* (University of Minnesota Press, 1993), p. 120.
28. Krutnik, *op. cit.*, p. 138; italics mine.
29. Walter Kerr, *The Silent Clowns* (Da Capo Press, 1980), p. 92.
30. James Agee, "Comedy's Greatest Era" in Rickman, *op. cit.*, p. 16.
31. *Ibid.*, p. 25.

Chapter 1

1. Stanley Cavell, *The World Viewed*, Enlarged Edition (Harvard University Press, Cambridge, Massachusetts and London, England, 1979), p. 37.
2. Maurice Merleau-Ponty, "The Film and the New Psychology" in *Sense and Nonsense* (Northwestern University Press, 1964, trans. Hubert L. Dreyfus & Patricia A. Dreyfus), pp. 48–59.
3. Merleau-Ponty, *op. cit.*, pp. 52–53.
4. Walter Kerr, *The Silent Clowns* (Da Capo Press, 1980), p. 74.
5. Henri Bergson, "Laughter" in Wylie Sypher (ed.), *Comedy: "An Essay on Comedy" by George Meredith and "Laughter" by Henri Bergson* (Johns Hopkins University Press, Baltimore and London, 1991), p. 97.
6. Cavell, *op. cit.*, p. 37.
7. René Descartes, "The Passions of the Soul, Part I" in Margaret D. Wilson (ed.), *The Essential Descartes* (Meridian 1969), pp. 357–8.
8. Bergson, "Laughter" in Sypher (ed.), *op. cit.*, p. 84.
9. Maurice Merleau-Ponty, *Phenomenology of Perception* (Routledge 2002), p. 101.
10. Descartes, "Correspondence with Princess Elisabeth" in Wilson (ed.), *op. cit.*, p. 379.

Chapter 2

1. See, for example, the discussion by John Gibbs on the use of framing in the train gag at the end of *One Week* (1921). Buster and wife give up pulling and pushing their entire house across some railway tracks and brace themselves for the inevitable collision with the train fast approaching in the background. To their surprise, and ours, the train whistles past leaving the house intact … only for another train to appear from *behind* the camera on another track and smash into the house after all. Gibbs notes this gag as a reminder by Keaton that "the frame is only a selective view of a wider fictional world." Of course, the gag's use of misleading perspective/trajectory lines also foregrounds the deceptiveness of the part of the world we *can* see. John Gibbs, *Mise-en-scène: Film Style and Interpretation* (Wallflower, London and New York, 2003), pp. 22–26.
2. As pointed out by George Adam Wead, the use of the far-shot, evocatively termed Keaton's "hieroglyphic range," is more prevalent in Keaton's earlier short films than in his later features which more regularly employ close and mid-shots. George Adam Wead, *Buster Keaton and the Dynamics of Visual Wit* (Northwestern University PhD thesis, 1973), p. 307.
3. One of the few in-depth discussions of Keaton's early work, Gabriella Oldham's book *Keaton's Silent Shorts* (Southern Illinois University Press, Carbondale and Edwardsville, 1996) has been useful in my thinking about these films. Despite a sometimes rather schematic treatment and a tendency to too-readily attribute "emotional" import to Keaton's style, its moment-by-moment analysis importantly considers the place of specific sequences within the patterns of each film.

4. Gilberto Perez stresses the way Keaton's world is "ruled by the implacable neatness of Newton's laws of mechanics." The same quality of neatness might be noted in Keaton's formal arrangement of space. Gilberto Perez, *The Material Ghost: Films and Their Medium* (Johns Hopkins University Press, 1998), p. 100.

5. The film thereby offers ample support for William Rothman's proposal that "his secret wish to be a viewer is at the heart of Keaton's comedy." William Rothman, *The "I" of the Camera: Essays in Film Criticism, History, and Aesthetics* (Cambridge University Press, 1988), p. 49.

6. Kerr discusses the recurrence of a narrative figure whereby Buster's selfmade fortune is swiftly and unforeseeably reversed, as if by Fate. Walter Kerr, *The Silent Clowns* (Da Capo Press, 1980), pp. 145–8. A "U-turn" motif also frequently recurs in Keaton's comedy, and often in association with just such a reversal of fortune.

7. As Cavell points out, Keaton is "at home everywhere and nowhere," a condition allowed for by the fact of film's tendency to "discover at any moment the endless contigency of the individual human's placement in the world." (Interestingly, Cavell finds Chaplin to inhabit the same condition.) Stanley Cavell, *The World Viewed: Enlarged Edition* (Harvard University Press, Cambridge, Massachusetts and London, England, 1979), pp. 181–2.

8. In a related vein, J.P. Lebel writes: "Buster Keaton's films provide the meeting ground for man and the world, and show this meeting in a comedy and ethic of action; encountering the world on physical and spatial terms, man appears, as he has appeared throughout history, in his most naked, elemental form." J.P. Lebel, *Buster Keaton* (A. Zwemmer Ltd, London 1967, trans. P.D. Stovin), p. 32.

9. Kerr explores Keaton's employment of the camera's potentially deceptive recording of depth in a chapter entitled "Keaton: Exploring the Gap Between Life and Lens." Kerr, *op. cit.*, pp. 135–142.

10. The comic materialisation of Buster's face behind bars is the first in a series of ways in which he is bestowed with the appearance of criminality: moments later Buster throws a horseshoe behind him for some much-needed luck, striking a cop who takes it for an aerial assault, and later still a gangster uses Buster's body for cover in a shootout against the police, then hands Buster the pistol to fit him up once again. As in *The Paleface*, identity is not organic but externally contrived.

Chapter 3

1. Quoted in William Cahn, *Harold Lloyd's World of Comedy* (George Allen & Unwin Ltd, 1966), pp. 144–5.

2. James Naremore, *Acting in the Cinema* (Berkeley: University of California Press, 1988), p. 86.

3. In an important passage on Chaplin, Stanley Cavell writes about the relationship between the boiled-boot episode and the equally famous dance-of-the-rolls sequence: "… in the one case a shoe is treated as a food (a case of dire necessity), in the other a food is treated as a shoe (a case of dire luxury); in both, his imagination gives habitation to his ecstasy and to his grief … Chaplin shows [the conditions under which a human being may be capable of happiness] to be those of free imagination, especially the imagination of happiness itself—an ability to gather your spirits no matter what has happened to them…" (Stanley Cavell, "What Becomes of Things on Film?" in *Themes Out of School: Effects and Causes* (University of Chicago Press, Chicago and London, 1988), p. 176.

4. Charles Chaplin, *My Autobiography* (The Bodley Head, 1964), pp. 154 and 156.

5. From "The Painter of Modern Life," in Charles Baudelaire, *Selected Writings on Art and Literature*, trans. P.E. Charvet (Penguin, 1992 [1863]), pp. 423–4.

6. In *The World Viewed*, Stanley Cavell interprets this text by Baudelaire as an "anticipation of film" — that is, as heralding a modern way of viewing the world which film would go on to provide more concretely — and this interpretation provides Cavell the opportunity to discuss the relationship between body and clothes in movies: "In paintings and in the theater, clothes reveal a person's character and his station, also his body and its attitudes. The clothes *are* the body, as the expression is the face. In movies, clothes conceal; hence they conceal something separate from them; the something is therefore empirically there to be unconcealed." Stanley Cavell, *The World Viewed: Enlarged Edition* (Harvard University Press, 1979), p. 43. Cavell's assertion of the inherent separateness of body and clothes on film may chime when considering Keaton, but less so with Chaplin, as I argue above. Indeed, the very phrase Cavell uses to describe theatre — "the clothes *are* the body, as the expression is the face" — seems to me to suit Chaplin very well, regardless of the fact that his clothes are technically divisible from his body. Chaplin's moustache is also divisible from him — but this fact doesn't make it any less a part of his body....

7. Tom Dardis, for example, writes: "Harold's development of his glasses character was a process of rediscovering himself: *he became an actor again*— what he had always wanted to be — not just another slapstick comedian in the shadow of Chaplin." (Italics author's own) — Tom Dardis, *Harold Lloyd: The Man on the Clock* (Penguin Books, 1984), p. 50. Douglas McCaffrey (*Three Classic Silent Screen Comedies Starring Harold Lloyd*, Associated University Press, 1976) and Walter Kerr (*The Silent Clowns*, Da Capo Press, 1990) similarly place importance on this costuming development towards an understanding of Lloyd's comedic persona.

8. Dardis, *op. cit.*, p. 102.

Chapter 4

1. Henri Bergson, "Laughter" in Wylie Sypher (ed.), *Comedy* (Johns Hopkins University Press, Baltimore and London, 1991, trans. Fred Rothwell), p. 79.

2. James Agee, "Comedy's Greatest Era" in *Agee on Film* (Peter Owen Ltd, 1967), p. 15.

3. Tom Gunning proposes that Keaton exhibits an "identification with the mechanical" which, he argues, reflects an essential ambivalence in 1920s' attitudes towards modernity, which "teeters between the utopian possibilities of the machine man so celebrated by the Russian Constructivists and the pliant automatism desired by Henry Ford and Frederick W. Taylor." Gunning goes on to imply that Keaton's films embody something of a critique of the dehumanising potential of the machine age, a claim I fail to see fully justified. Tom Gunning, "Buster Keaton, or the work of comedy in the age of mechanical reproduction," in Frank Krutnik (ed.): *Hollywood Comedians, The Film Reader* (Routledge 2003).

4. Karl Marx and Fredrich Engels, *The Communist Manifesto* (Penguin, 1985), p. 87.

5. This seems a perfect example of Bergson's insight that laughter results from the appearance of "something mechanical encrusting of the living" (Bergson, *op. cit.*, p. 84). An interesting note of discord may be heard to sound here between Bergson and Marx. Bergson argues that the presentation of "mechanical inelasticity" is laughable because of the way laughter performs the function of a social corrective — that is, we laugh at what we are not supposed to be: an inflexible automaton. However, the implication of Marx's comment (and of Chaplin's comedy) is that this is precisely what industrial society *does* demand of us (to become "an appendage of the machine").

6. Marx and Engels, *op. cit.*, p. 87.

Chapter 5

1. My appreciation here is greatly indebted to Charles Barr's book, *Laurel and Hardy* (Studio Vista Ltd., 1968), which allows us to recognise, without ponderous or overweighted analysis, how Stan and Ollie offer "in so clear a form so much of the human condition: pain and joy, authority and subversion, aspiration and disaster, generosity and ill-will, with the directness of allegory." *Ibid.*, p. 6.

2. Stanley Cavell, "Film in the University" in *Pursuits of Happiness: The Hollywood Comedy of Remarriage* (Harvard University Press, Cambridge, Massachusetts, and London, England, 1997), pp. 271–2.

3. The smallness and simplicity of their world is underscored by the use of shallow focus to depict actions that often occur along a single lateral plane; by the general sparsity of extraneous characters; and by the sense of this being a world defined by the task in hand, and by the tools used to pursue that task.

4. Gilberto Perez, *The Material Ghost: Films and Their Medium* (Johns Hopkins University Press, 1998), p. 100.

5. Stanley Cavell, *Pursuits of Happiness: The Hollywood Comedy of Remarriage* University Press, Cambridge, Massachusetts, and London, England, 1997), p. 2. (Emphases in original.) The study includes readings of *The Lady Eve* (1941), *It Happened One Night* (1934), *Bringing Up Baby*, *The Philadelphia Story* (1940), *His Girl Friday* (1940), *Adam's Rib* (1949), and *The Awful Truth* (1937).

6. *Ibid.*, p. 88.

7. *Ibid.*, pp. 126–7.

Chapter 6

1. The terms Imaginary and Symbolic are employed in Lacanian psychoanalysis to distinguish between two distinct phases in a child's development, the first before and the latter after the so-called mirror stage and the acquisition of language. Prior to recognising a distinction between subject and object that is stressed in language, the child caught up in the realm of the Imaginary imagines itself to be omnipotent and at one with the world around it. Interestingly, a marked wordlessness characterises those sporadic moments when both Stan Laurel and Jerry Lewis perform incredible physical feats: Stan's lighting of his thumb like a cigarette lighter in *Way Out West* (1937), for instance, or Jerry setting out chairs in a vast auditorium in a matter of seconds in *The Bellboy* (1960).

2. Michel Chion, *The Voice in Cinema* (Columbia University Press, 1999, trans. Claudia Gorbman), p. 125.

3. *Ibid.*, p. 128. (Italics in original.)

4. The film is *Annie Hall* (1977).

5. Charlie Chaplin, "Pantomime and Comedy," *The New York Times*, 25 January 1931, reprinted in David Robinson, *Charlie Chaplin: The Art of Comedy* (Thames and Hudson, 1996), p. 121.

6. Although Charlie does mouth words (and we see the opening sentence on a title card: "Now Goliath was a big man — "), the body takes over where language left off, and we perceive his intervention as pre-eminently physical rather than verbal. The silence of the film's world can be seen here as giving a prominence to his actions that reflects the stunned attention of the congregation.

7. Slavoj Žižek offers a different interpretation of Chaplin's suspicion of dialogue that is derived from Lacanian psychoanalysis, writing about the voice as an "intrusion": "It is the voice which corrupts the innocence of the silent burlesque, of this pre–Oedipal, oral-

anal paradise.... The advent of the voice, of the talking film, introduces a certain duality into Chaplin's universe: an uncanny split ... Chaplin's well-known aversion to sound is thus not to be dismissed as a simple, nostalgic commitment to a silent paradise; it reveals a far deeper than usual knowledge (or at least presentiment) of the disruptive power of the voice, of the fact that the voice functions as a foreign body, as a kind of parasite introducing a radical split: the advent of the Word throws the human animal off balance and makes of him a ridiculous, impotent figure, gesticulating and striving desperately for a lost balance." Slavoj Žižek, *Enjoy Your Symptom! Jacques Lacan in Hollywood and out* (Routledge: New York and London, 1992), pp. 1–2. Such an interpretation is fascinating, although perhaps overeager: the "uncanny split" (or doubling) found in *The Great Dictator* is present also in silent Chaplin films such as *The Idle Class*, whilst it might be tough to sustain the argument that the rather forbidding world of *The Immigrant* (1916) or the mannered social world of *The Adventurer* (1917) constitute an "oral-anal paradise." Moreover, the ridiculous, impotent, desperately gesticulating figure Žižek describes reminds me far more of Jerry Lewis than of Charlie Chaplin.

8. I am indebted to Neil Brand and the Tootin Orchestra for their terrific live accompaniment of the film at a screening during the Bristol Slapstick Silent Comedy Festival (13th–16th January 2005).

9. Alan Dale uses the phrase "verbal slapstick," as I am using it, to refer to "dialogue performed at a breakneck clip," but extends it to include any or all of the following impressive list of "characteristic gags": "the sarcastic aside, the comeback ... insipid verbosity ... orotundity ... one-liners, puns, vivid slang, outrageous metaphors, double entendres, non-sequiturs, malapropisms, mispronunciations, getting names wrong, and foreign accents." Offering films directed by Preston Sturges, Frank Capra and Howard Hawks as prime examples, Dale pushes the analogy, rather too far in my opinion, to encompass almost all forms of verbal wit. Alan Dale, *Comedy Is a Man in Trouble: Slapstick in American Movies* (University of Minnesota Press, 2000), pp. 5–6.

10. Transcribed (painstakingly!) by Alex Clayton, with the help of multiple re-viewings.

11. Raymond Durgnat, *The Crazy Mirror: Hollywood Comedy and the American Image* (Faber & Faber Ltd., 1969), p. 234.

12. Frank Krutnik, *Reinventing Jerry Lewis* (Smithsonian Institution Press, Washington and London, 2000), p. 138.

13. It is certainly not through lack of trying. In *The Disorderly Orderly* (1965), Nurse Higgins, maddened by Jerry's blunders on the hospital ward, even finds cause to tell him to "try hard not to try so hard" — an instruction that Jerry will try hard to obey. Steven Shaviro sees the Lewis figure as an "unconscious anarchist," "not in spite of, but because of, his hyperconformism: he disseminates chaos in the course of earnestly trying to do what bosses, psychoanalysts, media specialists, and other technicians of normalizing power want him to do." Steven Shaviro, *The Cinematic Body* (University of Minnesota Press, 1993), p. 110.

Chapter 7

1. Maurice Merleau-Ponty, *Phenomenology of Perception* (Routledge, 2002), pp. 106–9.

2. The effect must have been achieved through a process of double exposure, yet the result is so seamless that there is no residual sense of imposition.

3. Stanley Cavell, *Pursuits of Happiness: The Hollywood Comedy of Remarriage* (Harvard University Press, 2000), p. 122.

4. Of course, the task of appearing to do nothing in this sequence actually requires a

great deal of acrobatic skill; Dorothy Sebastien's proficient performance of unconsciousness is as crucial to the effect as Keaton's careful manoeuvrings.

5. The camera's sustained viewpoint through the imaginary fourth wall brings out a resemblance to a theatre stage and so accentuates the feeling of a vaudeville performance (or perhaps a puppet show), importantly recalling the earlier scene in which Buster is himself immobilised on-stage, transfixed by the woman's beauty.

6. He adds that Lewis's *The Nutty Professor* (1963) is concerned with the problem of how to be reconciled "to oneself." Raymond Durgnat, *The Crazy Mirror: Hollywood Comedy and the American Image* (Faber & Faber Ltd., 1969).

7. Molly Haskell, in *From Reverence to Rape*, is less generous to Laurel and Hardy, seeing them as "unequivocally antifemale": "Of all the silent comedians, Laurel and Hardy are perhaps the most threatening to women, as they combine physical ruination with misogyny. One epicene and gross, the other emaciated, they are an aesthetic offense. With their disaster-prone bodies and their exclusive relationship that not only shuts out women but questions their very necessity, they constitute a two-man wrecking team of female — that is, civilized and bourgeois — society." Molly Haskell, *From Reverence to Rape: The Treatment of Women in the Movies* (New English Library, 1974), pp. 66–7 Whilst I often find Haskell stimulating and astute, I don't see how physical ruination and the destruction of bourgeois society constitute an assault on women. It is true that their wives are possessive dragons, occasionally armed with shotguns, but consider just some of the characteristics Laurel and Hardy seem to associate specifically with men: arrogance, fickleness, clumsiness, pomposity, idiocy and ineptitude, not to mention an uncontrollably bad temper....

8. Judith Butler argues that gender identity is performative, having "no ontological status apart from the various acts which constitute its reality," but that these bodily gestures "create the illusion of an interior and organizing gender core." Drag, she argues, "effectively mocks the expressive model of gender [that is, the idea that gestures express a gendered 'essence'] and the notion of a true gender identity." The performance of drag "avows the distinctness" of sex and gender, and "dramatizes the cultural mechanism of their fabricated unity." Moreover, "in imitating gender, drag implicitly reveals the imitative structure of gender itself — as well as its contingency ... laughter emerges in the realization that all along the original was derived." Judith Butler, *Gender Trouble: Feminism and the Subversion of Identity* (Routledge, 1990), pp. 136–139. We might see *Some Like It Hot* as a feature-length exploration of this thesis.

Chapter 8

1. Whilst physical pain is not of central interest in Chaplin's comedy, there are brief and daring moments, notably in *The Tramp* (1915), *The Adventurer* (1917) and *The Great Dictator* (1940), when the sudden appearance of realistic injury peppers the presentation of cartoonish slapstick. As Walter Kerr writes, "There was an unspoken law of silent comedy under which no one ever got hurt (as Chaplin is, briefly, floating unconscious during *The Adventurer* (the image is immediately false and unattractive, a violation of the form's promise." Walter Kerr, *The Silent Clowns* (Da Capo Press, 1980), p. 63.

2. *Jackass* began as a series on MTV in 2000, and achieved such cult popularity that a feature-length film (bearing great resemblance to the TV series, but with an evidently bigger budget and more extreme stunts) gained a cinema release in 2002. Regular performers include Johnny Knoxville, Chris Pontius, Bam Margera and Steve-O.

3. Keaton hides the pain, however, rather than flaunting it. When he reportedly broke

his neck performing in *Sherlock Jr.* (1924), Keaton continued the take to its planned end. Incredibly, this very take was used in the final film, but there is no hint whatsoever of the agony that Keaton must have been in.

4. Jerry explains his neurosis to a fellow worker in the hospital Photo Room, standing in the dark next to a projector throwing light onto a screen. By process of association, the condition is linked with the very workings of cinema, and with the ordinary condition of the cinema viewer who identifies with figures in pain.

Chapter 9

1. There is an invisible (or almost invisible) match cut between Charley's exit and entrance, whilst the wife stands at the door.

2. Ludwig Wittgenstein, *Philosophical Investigations* (Blackwell, 2003, trans. G.E.M. Anscombe), p. 152.

3. Tom Gunning points out the montage between human and animal characteristics in this sequence, and the resultant composite body which Gunning posits as a distinctly modernist feature of Chaplin's work. Tom Gunning, "Chaplin and the Body of Modernity" (as yet unpublished paper, delivered at The Charles Chaplin Conference, London College of Communication, 21–24 July 2005).

4. In a self-reflexive meditation on the nature of cinema itself, *Sherlock Jr.* suggests the body-on-film to be at once ethereal *and* physical.

5. The monstrousness of the Jekyll-figure is signalled in our first sight of Lewis as the buck-toothed Kelp, arising from beneath the flattened door of his blown-up chemistry lab, like a vampire awakening from his coffin.

Conclusion

1. This claim evidently shares some common ground with Stanley Cavell's suggestion that "Keaton's silent absorption with things" fits Heidegger's phenomenological account of "the worldhood of the world" in *Being and Time* (see the chapter entitled "Body and Frame" for Cavell's summary of this account).

2. Of course, laughter may be another physical process that can unite an audience into a sense of a "shared" body; but such claims are merely conjecture and move away from the main subject of this book, which is the body *in* (not the body as affected by) Hollywood slapstick.

3. Peter Berger, *Redeeming Laughter: The Comic Dimension of Human Experience* (Walter de Gruyter & Co, 1997), p. 209. Italics in original.

Bibliography

Agee, James. "Comedy's Greatest Era." In Gregg Rickman (ed.), *The Film Comedy Reader*. New York: Limelight, 2001.

Bakhtin, Mikhail. *Rabelais and His World*. Trans. Helene Iswolsky. Bloomington: Indiana University Press, 1984

Barr, Charles. *Laurel and Hardy*. London: Studio Vista, 1968.

Baudelaire, Charles. "The Painter of Modern Life." In Charles Baudelaire, *Selected Writings on Art and Literature*. Trans. P.E. Charvet. New York: Penguin, 1992,

Bazin, Andr(. *What Is Cinema?* Trans. Hugh Gray. Berkeley: University of California Press, 1967.

Berger, Peter. *Redeeming Laughter: The Comic Dimension of Human Experience*. Berlin: Walter de Gruyter, 1997.

Bergson, Henri. "Laughter." In Wylie Sypher (ed.), *Comedy*. Trans. Fred Rothwell. Baltimore: Johns Hopkins University Press, 1991.

Butler, Judith. *Gender Trouble: Feminism and the Subversion of Identity*. London: Routledge, 1990.

Cahn, William. *Harold Lloyd's World of Comedy*. London: George Allen & Unwin, 1966.

Cavell, Stanley. *Cavell on Film*. Ed. William Rothman. Albany: State University of New York Press, 2005.

_____. *Pursuits of Happiness: The Hollywood Comedy of Remarriage*. Cambridge, Mass.: Harvard University Press, 1997.

_____. "What Becomes of Things on Film?" In Stanley Cavell, *Themes Out of School: Effects and Cause*. Chicago: University of Chicago Press, 1988.

_____. *The World Viewed: Enlarged Edition*. Cambridge, Mass.: Harvard University Press, 1979.

Chaplin, Charlie. "Pantomime and Comedy." *The New York Times*, 25 January 1931. Reprinted in David Robinson, *Charlie Chaplin: The Art of Comedy*. London: Thames and Hudson, 1996.

Chaplin, Charles. *My Autobiography*. London: Bodley Head, 1964.

Chion, Michel. *The Voice in Cinema*. Trans. Claudia Gorbman. New York: Columbia University Press, 1999.

Dale, Alan. *Comedy Is a Man in Trouble: Slapstick in American Movies*. St. Paul: University of Minnesota Press, 2000.

223

Bibliography

Dardis, Tom. *Harold Lloyd: The Man on the Clock*. New York: Penguin, 1984.

Descartes, René. "The Passions of the Soul, Part I" and "Correspondence with Princess Elisabeth." In René Descartes, *The Essential Descartes*. Ed. Margaret Wilson. New York: Meridian, 1969.

Durgnat, Raymond. *The Crazy Mirror: Hollywood Comedy and the American Image*. London: Faber & Faber, 1969.

Freud, Sigmund. *The Joke and Its Relation to the Unconscious*. Trans. Joyce Crick. New York: Penguin, 2002.

Gibbs, John. *Mise-en-scene: Film Style and Interpretation*. London: Wallflower, 2003.

Gunning, Tom. "Buster Keaton, or the Work of Comedy in the Age of Mechanical Reproduction." In Frank Krutnik (ed.), *Hollywood Comedians, The Film Reader*. London: Routledge, 2003.

_____. "Chaplin and the Body of Modernity." Paper delivered at the Charles Chaplin Conference, London College of Communication, 21–24 July 2005. Copy forwarded by kind permission of the author.

Haskell, Molly. *From Reverence to Rape: The Treatment of Women in the Movies*. London: New English Library, 1974.

Kerr, Walter. *The Silent Clowns*. New York: Da Capo, 1980.

Klevan, Andrew. *Film Performance: From Achievement to Appreciation*. London: Wallflower, 2005.

Krutnik, Frank. *Reinventing Jerry Lewis*. Washington, D.C.: Smithsonian Institution Press, 2000.

Lebel, J.P. *Buster Keaton*. Trans. P.D. Stovin. London: A. Zwemmer, 1967.

Marx, Karl, and Engels, Fredrich. *The Communist Manifesto*. New York: Penguin, 1985.

Mast, Gerald. *The Comic Mind: Comedy and the Movies*. Chicago: University of Chicago Press, 1973.

McCaffrey, Douglas. *Three Classic Silent Screen Comedies Starring Harold Lloyd*. Cranbury, N.J.: Associated University Presses, 1976.

Merleau-Ponty, Maurice. "The Film and the New Psychology." In Maurice Merleau-Ponty, *Sense and Nonsense*. Trans. Hubert L. Dreyfus & Patricia A. Dreyfus. Evanston, Ill.: Northwestern University Press, 1964.

_____. *Phenomenology of Perception*. Trans. Colin Smith. London: Routledge, 2002.

Naremore, James. *Acting in the Cinema*. Berkeley: University of California Press, 1988.

Oldham, Gabriella. *Keaton's Silent Shorts*. Carbondale: Southern Illinois University Press, 1996.

Panofsky, Erwin. "Style and Medium in the Motion Pictures." In Gerald Mast and Marshall Cohen (eds.), *Film Theory and Criticism: Introductory Readings*. New York: Oxford University Press, 1979.

Paul, William. "Charles Chaplin and the Annals of Anality." In Andrew Horton, *Comedy/Cinema/Theory*. Berkeley: University of California Press, 1991.

Perez, Gilberto. *The Material Ghost: Films and Their Medium*. Baltimore: Johns Hopkins University Press, 1998.

Robinson, David. *Charlie Chaplin: The Art of Comedy*. London: Thames and Hudson, 1996.

Rothman, William. *The 'I' of the Camera: Essays in Film Criticism, History, and Aesthetics*. Cambridge, England: Cambridge University Press, 1988.

Shaviro, Steven. *The Cinematic Body*. St. Paul: University of Minnesota Press, 1993.

Bibliography

Wead, George Adam. *Buster Keaton and the Dynamics of Visual Wit.* Ph.D. diss., Northwestern University, 1973.

Wittgenstein, Ludwig. *Philosophical Investigations.* Trans. G.E.M. Anscombe.London: Blackwell, 2003.

Žižek, Slavoj. *Enjoy Your Symptom! Jacques Lacan in Hollywood and Out.* London: Routledge, 1992.

/

Index

227

Index

Index